"Interviews"

Brian Wallace

"Interviews"

© 2020 by Brian Wallace

ISBN-13:   978-0-9913556-6-2
ISBN-10:   0-9913556-6-0

Contents:

Scripture References
Following Each Interview

"Interview" 1
John the Baptizer

I hate having to meet you in this cell. You deserve better than to be locked up like this.

Deserve? The coming wrath is what we deserve.

That sounds like something you would say.

That's one of the benefits of telling the truth… you don't have to change your message. What I declared before I declare again: Turn back to God. The kingdom is at hand!

I wanted to ask you about that. You were preaching the same thing two thousand years ago, yet we are still here. Was your timing way off? What happened?

What happened? Only everything! The Lamb of God – the one I was sent to prepare the way for, the one whose sandals I am not worthy to untie – he was here! We saw him. He accomplished his purpose, laid down his life, defeated sin and death, and rose again. What happened? Everything!

Then why isn't it over? Why haven't we received the promise?

Listen! You are expecting things to unfold a certain way, but I tell you that time is different than you think. The axe is already at the root of the tree. Looking back it will be clear, but know this… Those who heard me then have indeed seen the promise fulfilled and the warning realized. The end came for each of them, and quickly. Now I speak to you. Avoid the flames. Produce good fruit. Live for God!

That kind of preaching doesn't go over very well today. People do not like to be shouted at.

Oh, it is not the shouting. People are fine with shouting, so long as it is things we want to hear. It is conviction that we do not like. It is the call to surrender the self that we have a problem with. It was the same then as it is now. That is why they locked me up.

Because you made them feel guilty?

Because I exposed the guilt that was already there! When you declare the truth, the world will eventually try to silence you. My arrest was no surprise. All is well.

All is well? You are in prison with no chance of release.

Release... as if man has any say over that! Hear and understand - I was set free from the beginning!

I hate to be the bearer of bad news, but you never make it out of this cage. Those iron bars are real.

That's true. The body can be captured. How much more the soul! Consider this: you are free to walk up those steps and go about your business. Yet I am free – even in these chains - to go about God's business! Which is the greater freedom?

What does that mean?

When circumstances change - when you cannot go and do what you want - does your freedom remain?

I don't see how it could. How can you be free if you cannot do what you want?

What a weak freedom! It can be taken away in an instant. A change in season, a sickness or an injury, poverty or an unjust law - all of these can destroy that kind of freedom. There is a deeper freedom! It is that freedom found when you are walking in step with the Spirit of God, spending yourself doing exactly what He created you to do. Sickness, poverty, prison, even death; none of them can touch that freedom.

How can you tell the difference?

When God allows difficult seasons, when you are "in chains for the Gospel" – whatever those chains may be – then you will discover whether your freedom is real or if your "freedom" was a prison all along.

And if I find out that I have been chasing the wrong kind of freedom? If I am living a fruitless life, trapped in a dungeon of my own design, what then?

The Lamb holds the keys. Follow him out.

Scriptural Basis for "Interview" 1

**Luke 3
Matthew 3
John 1
Revelation 1:18**

"Interview" 2
Eve

Wow! Pardon my saying so, but you are perfect!

… I wish I was.

Come on. You're being modest. I've seen many beautiful women, but you… you are stunning!

I should be. In the story of creation, I was the final piece. You might say that I was God's finishing touch.

You certainly are! I can't even begin to describe you. I don't see a flaw!

There wasn't. Trust me, I know what it is to be flawless. There is a difference now.

I suppose I do see something… in your eyes. There is sorrow there. Terrible shadows.

Yes…

Where does that come from?

Surely you know. Even those who understand nothing else about me usually picture me eating that apple.

Except it wasn't an apple, was it?

No.

And those shadows in your eyes are about much more than a piece of fruit...

Of course.

Was it being kicked out of Eden? Is that what haunts you?

No. We would have been fine outside the garden.

What then?

Have you ever had a moment, just a flash, when everything made sense? When you felt alive in the deepest of ways? One of those moments when all is right with the world and your life is so rich that you can't hide your smile? Have you ever been in awe of how good things are and felt your heart flooded with peace, delighting in the pure and unbridled joy that you know must be coming straight from God? Where love is the only law you have to follow and the entire world longs to be shaped by your commands?

Not really.

Well, that was our normal.

Fascinating.

7

It was more than fascinating. It is what you ache for and don't even recognize; what you truly need but won't admit to your own heart. But you feel it. You feel it as a hunger in your soul, an unsettled place inside that you can never quite put your finger on. And when this whole world seems undeniably broken and unsatisfying... when, even though you've never lived anywhere else, you feel overwhelmingly homesick... you are missing what we had.

The garden was that perfect?

No. Not the garden. Him!

You mean God?

He was what filled us up. Both Adam and I could find ourselves in Him. I had no other women to talk to until I had my daughters, but that part of myself was already there in God. Adam found the same. There was man - male and female - hidden inside God. So Adam had a brother and a sister and a father and a mother and a friend. And I had the same. Oh, Adam and I were perfectly suited for each other, but it was God who wove us together. It was God who made us complete.

And you lost that...

Yes.

That must have been awful.

You have no idea. All other grief pales in comparison.

I feel like we still experience some of that now – some of that grief... that emptiness and anxiety.

You do. The shadows you see in my eyes are there in yours as well... You know that loss of closeness with God, and seeing what that loss does to my kids breaks my heart.

To your kids?

Yes. All of you. I'm so sorry...

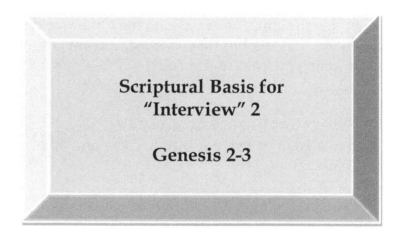

Scriptural Basis for "Interview" 2

Genesis 2-3

"Interview" 3
Balaam's Donkey

So you're the talking donkey, huh?

No. I'm not.

Good. Let me start with a question that I've wondered ever since reading your story. Are all donkeys able to talk? I mean, I've never heard one speak before, but I've never spent a whole lot of time hanging out with them either.

Let me get this straight... you're asking me if the world is full of donkeys that talk but that we all stay silent around humans to keep you from finding out?

Yes.

OK, I'm gonna go now. I've got stuff to carry and other donkeys to not talk to.

Wait. I'm sorry. Don't go. I have a better question...

It better be.

Apart from telling your master to stop beating you, what is something that you would say to people if God opened your mouth and enabled you to speak one more time?

That's a much better question. I think I would tell people how lucky they are to be loved by a God who hides himself from them.

That doesn't make sense.

Neither do talking donkeys.

Good point. Still, I don't get why it would be good for God to conceal himself.

That's because you are like Balaam. You still can't see. But one day you will. One day it will all be clear, and you will be amazed at the deep, deep relationship that God forged with you during your wanderings and your groping along by faith. On that day you will finally discover how valuable it was each time you trusted God instead of your eyes, how incredibly important it was to choose to believe that God's heart is good. It hurts right now, the growing you are doing. It's not easy. But you are currently in the middle of a story that is bigger than you ever imagined. Free, eternal, and powerful... nothing on earth compares to the love being built between God and mankind. Not God and donkeys. Not even God and angels. God and man. You men and women are the beloved of God! That is what you cannot see yet – how much He truly loves you. And the rest of creation, this talking donkey included, is in awe of your place in His heart.

How do you know all this?

It's obvious. All of creation can see it. All except you.

Why? Why are donkeys allowed to see what man cannot?

Because God knows we're not going to say anything.

But if you could?

"Lucky man!" That's what I would say.

Scriptural Basis for "Interview" 3

**Numbers 22
Song of Songs**

"Interview" 4
Peter

I usually give people a few warm up questions. You know... to let them ease in.

Thanks, but we can skip all that. The fish are waiting.

So just let loose?

Cast away.

What was your hardest day? Was it when Jesus looked you in the eye and called you Satan?

No, that was just a smack on the beak. I needed it. Besides, you have to remember; that was the same day he called me 'Rock' and said he would build his church on that rock and that the gates of Hell would not defeat us. All in all, that day was pretty good.

The hardest then?

The hardest was Saturday.

Saturday?

Well, Saturday is what you call it. To us it was the Sabbath.

The day of rest, right?

Usually. But not that day. Not for us. Not for me.

Why not?

It was the day between.

Between?

We didn't know that's what it was at the time. If we had – if I had listened with a bit more faith – it wouldn't have been nearly as bad. But I didn't see it. I didn't realize it was the day between. For me it was the end.

The end of what?

The end of everything. That's how it felt. Doors locked. Every sound a threat. Hating yourself. Hating the world. There was no future. No meaning. No purpose to being alive or continuing to struggle. It was over. Hope was dead.

Oh, you're talking about the crucifixion...

We had followed him for three years. Saw him healing people just by touching them. Can you imagine actually witnessing that? Clouds vanishing from blind eyes so that they were able to see? Thousands of people eating from a handful of fish and a few loaves of bread? It was unreal. He called into a tomb and a dead man walked out, fully restored! No one had seen anything like this. Not since

Moses and Elijah. But here was this Jesus, giving commands to the skies and the seas, and the earth bowed in obedience. Even the spiritual forces that stood against us crumbled and fled at his approach. He changed the earth just by walking on it, and we saw it all.
Then he died.

Just like that?

Just like that. As if it was written that way and nothing in the world could stop it. The story was over. We had seen life. We had glimpsed the promise. We walked with God's Messiah and were expecting him to take his throne at any moment, to save Israel forever. We had entered Jerusalem to the crowds crying 'Hosanna' and laying their clothing on his path. Not even a week later it was over. He was dead, executed by the Romans at the request of our own leaders.

What was that like for you personally?

You asked about the hardest day of my life. That's when it began. Our teacher, our friend, our King – beaten beyond recognition and then hung up on a pole for the world to mock until he stopped breathing. Do you understand? The things we saw... he was changing the world! The hope of our people, the hope of the whole human race, God's promise in the flesh...! We watched that nailed to a cross, and we ran away and hid. I even denied that I knew him.

It's understandable. You were afraid for your life.

That doesn't matter. It doesn't change the fact that my Lord was dead and I was a coward. I remember hiding there in the dark, just wanting to die. There is a prophecy in Hosea that speaks of the people pleading for the hills to fall on them and for the mountains to cover them. That was my prayer that day. I longed to be buried by the mountains. It was the saddest, darkest day of my life. The day between.

Wow... OK, what about the best day of your life?

Amazingly enough, it was the day right after that! And every day since...

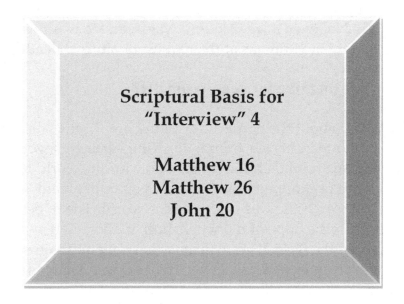

Scriptural Basis for
"Interview" 4

Matthew 16
Matthew 26
John 20

"Interview" 5
Jonah

Oh, you're here! That's great! I was a little worried you might take off in the opposite direction.

Oh! Shots fired. Very funny. You're a comedian then?

No, I just do interviews. Before we get started, why don't we go ahead and order our meal. Do you want the chicken or the fish?

Oh, I don't eat fish. I always spit them back out. I guess I'm kind of paying it forward.

Fair enough. Alright, question one... You get to write your own epitaph. What does it say?

"Just between me and you, I'm really glad it didn't chew..."

Hey, that's not bad! Did you just come up with that on the spot?

No. I had a lot of time to reflect while I was 'in the belly.' I've got a handful of pretty morbid one-liners saved up for dinner parties... and interviews.

I'd love to hear them, but first I'd like to ask you to give us something more valuable. If you could offer up one

nugget of wisdom that you gained through your journey, what would it be?

If I can only choose one?

Yes. The wisdom of Jonah distilled down to one phrase.

It's better to do it God's way the first time.

Isn't that the truth! And appropriate advice from the poster child of second chances. Which leads to our next question... There are Biblical accounts of other people who disobeyed God and were simply destroyed. Why do you think you got a second chance? Why didn't he just drown you and send someone more faithful?

Ouch. You don't mess around with your questions.

I was afraid if it wasn't direct enough you might dodge it and run.

Oh... wow.

Just teasing. You survived being inside a fish for three days. I figured you can take a little harassment.

I suppose that's true. Actually, my answer has a lot to do with those three days. There is plenty that can be learned from my story, but right there in the heart of it is the sign delivered by those three days.

The sign?

There are a handful of people whose lives provide direct prophetic revelations of God's bigger plan to save the world. I was blessed to be one of them. Why did I get a second chance? Because one: God is merciful. And two: I was a sign.

How exactly were you a sign?

Long after my time, Jesus gets accosted by a group of Pharisees who challenge his authority and demand a sign as proof. Now he could have easily performed any one of countless miracles to authenticate what he was claiming – and in fact he did exactly that while they were not around – but the truth is that he did not come to make peace on man's terms. He came to make peace on God's terms. So God did provide a sign, but He did it far enough ahead of time that the Pharisees weren't around yet to see it – that sign was me. I am the sign that was provided, hundreds of years in advance, to answer the challenge from the Pharisees.

Did they accept it?

No. They didn't even understand it, but he told the Pharisees plainly that 'the sign of the prophet Jonah' was the only sign they would receive.

And what did he mean by that?

In his own words? 'For as Jonah was three days and three nights in the belly of a huge fish, so the Son of Man will be three days and three nights in the heart of the earth.' Long before Jesus endured the tomb for our salvation, my time in the fish was a sign that it would happen, and even more, that it would end!

Oh wait!

That's right. I see that you get it. I was not a sign of the tomb. Any dead guy could have been that. My story is revolutionary because I got out! That is the miraculous part. Not that I was swallowed by death, but that I was set free. I was a sign, not of the tomb, but of the resurrection! That was the sign the Pharisees were given. That is the sign the world has been given.

So it wasn't just that he would be buried...

No. The story would be awful if it ended there. For all of us! But it didn't end there. Three days and nights I spent praying in that dark and horrid place, cut off from the light - separated from life itself! But inside that fish the Spirit of God not only saved me but also gave me the strength to proclaim what he would do. 'Salvation comes from the LORD,' I cried, 'You brought my life up from the pit.' I shouted these truths from the grave, and that is where he came to get me. That is where he comes to get all of us.

Of course! You didn't stay in that fish – because He wasn't going to stay in the tomb.

That's right. Praise God for that! And now you won't either! Trust me on this one... it's good to be out!

Scriptural Basis for
"Interview" 5

Jonah
Matthew 12

"Interview" 6
Martha

Who is older, you or Mary?

Well aren't you a cracked pot! You interview people for a living and you don't know that there are certain questions you do not ask a woman? How many people have you interviewed?

Not too many.

I can tell. Since you are clearly new at this, please do us both a favor and get right to the point, OK? I have people coming over and supper to prepare.

Yes, of course. Right away.

Well...?

Many of us are interested in the relationship between you and your sister.

Isn't that always how it is? Mary and Martha, Mary and Martha... never just Martha.

Does that bother you?

A little bit, yes. I am more than just a character in my sister's story. I have a story of my own, you know. But it often feels like all people see in me is the example of what not to do. Here is Mary, sitting peacefully at the Lord's feet, and there - witness the contrast - is her harried sister Martha, running around frantically and obsessing over her to-do list. Do you have any idea how that feels? Does anyone stop to find out what is in my heart?

Do you hate your sister?

Do I...? Of all the impertinent...! How dare you suggest...?

A moment ago you bemoaned the fact that no one asks about your heart. That's what I am doing. It's a tough question, but an honest one. Does Martha hate her sister?

- no... no, I don't hate my sister. I resent her sometimes, but most of that is just envy.

What are you envious of?

I'm not sure that is any of your business.

You're right. But if you really want to be more than just a character in Mary's story, you're going to have to tell yours - the good and the bad.

Fine. I suppose that makes sense. What was your question?

You mentioned being envious. Envious of what?

I don't know why I am sharing this... I worked so hard to get ready for Jesus to come for supper. I wanted everything to be perfect. I wanted him to be impressed. So I got it all prepared. Even after he arrived, I stayed busy trying to make sure everything was just right. But do you know who connected with him? Mary did. And how? By not doing anything more than simply enjoying his company. That is what I am envious of.

That she was able to connect with him so easily?

Yes. She didn't earn it. She just… listened. Sitting there so close to him, she didn't miss a word. And he saw her. I want that.

Didn't he see you as well?

Yes. I suppose he did. He knew exactly where my heart was. He knew how distracted and burdened I was.

What did you take away from that?

You know, I could see it once Jesus pointed it out. My sister - oh it used to make me so mad! – she would stop working and talk to people. Laugh with people. Cry with people. Seeing her put her load down used to infuriate me. Because let's be honest; there is a lot of work to do in this life. Without the work, dinner doesn't happen. And it's not like clothes wash themselves. But I also see now that there is a line we can cross. There is a level of busyness and anxiety that we can become trapped in, and I lived there.

What was it that had you trapped? Why couldn't you put the load down?

Because the world might end if you don't finish the chores! It's silly, I know, but that is where the heart goes sometimes. So you finish the chores. You cook and clean and make sure there is enough food. And then you look up and everyone is gone. You missed it. Life happened and you missed it. So you clear the table and do the dishes, promising yourself that you will pay more attention next time. But then life happens again and you have to do your part to make sure it happens the right way, and you never actually let it happen to you. I watched my sister from behind those bars. I watched her sitting at his feet, the water pitcher forgotten on the ground beside her. She was good at laying down the burden to make time for what was more important.

That's a nice transition; here comes your sister now. Mary, please come over and join us. I am interviewing Martha.

About what?

Her heart.

Oh, I want to hear!

Actually, we're going to wrap things up with one last question – for her sister.

Me?

Who knows her better than you do? Tell us... What should the world know about Martha's heart?

Oh Martha! ...How a faithful heart holds a family together! People know about her being busy and worried, but when it is time to gather, where does everyone show up? Our house. They come to our house and they are always fed. Their feet are always washed. Everyone is always taken care of. And why? My sister. She could worry less, of course. Jesus spoke to that clearly enough. And I do wish that she would let herself surrender once in a while to be present in important moments. But there is a price paid by those who serve, and Martha spent a lot of time making sure other people's needs were met. There is value in that, and I see it every time our house fills up. There is a reason they always come here.

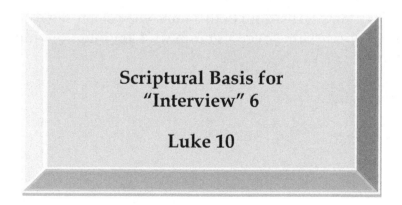

Scriptural Basis for "Interview" 6

Luke 10

"Interview" 7
Samson

How did you know she was the one?

I'm not sure. That's just how it was with me and women. I would see the right girl and that would be it. I always fell fast and hard. I guess I'm kind of a romantic.

Hahaha! A romantic. That's funny.

Why is that funny? You don't think I'm romantic?

No, I didn't mean it like that! Please sit back down. I'm sure you are terribly romantic. It's just that... that's not what most people know about you.

Of course not. Romance is only what initiates the journey. It's not what ends it. Not for me, anyway.

What does end it?

Betrayal. Then death. That's how the story goes, over and over again. Romance, then betrayal, then death.

That's how it went for you?

Twice. Almost three times.

You died twice?

No. The first time it was she who died.

You didn't...

What? Kill her? Of course not! What kind of man do you think I am? When it comes to wounds and women, I was always on the receiving end.

But you said the first one died...

Yeah – *they* killed her.

Who?

Her own people.

Why?

Revenge.

Revenge for what?

You ask a lot of questions.

That's my job. Why did they really kill her?

Because I burned their crops.

You burned their crops?

Well, technically the foxes burned their crops, but I was the one who tied their tails together and lit them on fire.

Oh, wow... I can't imagine what that looked like.

It was awesome.

I believe you.

Of course they weren't happy with what I had done, but instead of coming to see me like actual men, they went and burned my wife to death instead. Cowards!

What then? What did you do?

I did exactly what you imagine I did.

Which was?

Let's just say they won't be needing those crops anymore...

You killed them all?

All I could find. Their friends didn't like that, though, so they all got together and came looking for me. Probably because they couldn't find any more women to attack.

They hunted you down...

Of course not. They weren't that brave. They threatened my people instead and convinced them to hand me over.

And they did? Your own people handed you over?

Yeah. They did. They were kind of cowards too.

So they handed you over, and...?

And that is the fight you probably heard about. That one made the rounds. I even wrote a song about it. Say, you want to hear it?

No, thank y –

With a donkey's jawbone
I made donkeys of them
With a donkey's jawbone
I have killed a thousand men!

Hey, you have a really nice voice!

I told you I was a romantic.

Yes you did. And you were right about something else as well... I had heard about that fight before.

Because of my song?

No, it was your choice of weapon. A jawbone? Really?

It wasn't like there was a huge selection to choose from. When you are surrounded in the middle of an open field, you take what you can get. I gotta tell you, though, that jawbone actually handled pretty well.

Apparently so...

Say, I have a question for you... Have you ever fought in the Spirit of God before?

Can't say as I have.

Let me tell you, it's indescribable! You feel so strong! Uncontainably strong. And fast... I can't even tell you how fast I was! They came at me in waves, and in waves I sent them spinning toward the earth.

Be honest with me though... Were there really a thousand, or was that a bit of exaggeration; a little poetic hyperbole for your song?

Actually, it was probably closer to two thousand, but I don't like to brag.

Two thousand?

It gets hard to count after a while. The bodies start to pile up.

That's kind of gruesome.

They burned my wife to death.

Oh yeah... Well...

And they ended up gouging my eyes out, too.

31

I was going to ask you about that.

Worst pain I ever felt in my life. That moment when your eyeballs pop inside your head? You'll want to avoid that one if you can.

You're kind of a dark guy.

Well that happens. I'm a romantic, remember? That's where it leads sometimes.

How did being a romantic lead to having your eyes gouged out?

Oh, now I know you know this part of my story. Only a few Bible scholars can recount my honey riddle or sing my jawbone song from memory, but almost everyone has heard the one name that is eternally linked to mine. It's not my father's name, or my mother's. It's not the name of my country. It's not even the name of my God. It's hers…

Delilah.

Ungh…

It still gets you, huh?

I don't know if it's even her anymore. It's been so long that I can't really remember what she looks like. But she's gone, and I feel that every day. You remember what I said about having my eyes gouged out being the worst pain in my life? Scratch that. My eyes popping was terrible, but at least it was temporary. The pain she left me with... it doesn't heal. There's no scar – just a hole.

She broke you.

Into a million pieces. A thousand men couldn't do it.

But one woman...

It's my own fault. She proved over and over that I couldn't trust her, but I gave in.

Why do you think you gave in? Because you're a romantic?

No. I'm not going to cheapen it like that. I won't sit here and try to justify it. I failed. That's the truth.

Failed? How so?

I blame Delilah for betraying me, and she did, but it was nothing I hadn't already done to God. He gave me such power! Incredible strength! But I didn't use it for Him. That's my great confession. All of those exploits you read about – they were all about me. I did them for myself. Passionate? Yes. I certainly was. But there was supposed to be a purpose for all that passion and strength. I wasn't set apart from birth for no reason; I was supposed to lead my people and deliver them from the Philistines. God placed a great calling on my life, but I used his gifts to get what I wanted. I see that now, standing here without my eyes. It all gets so much clearer once it's over.

But didn't you begin to weaken Philistine control? Isn't that what you were supposed to do?

Maybe. I have no doubt that God accomplishes his plans no matter what. Still, I wonder... How much more would God have done through me if I had been less wrapped up in my own desires and more focused on His?

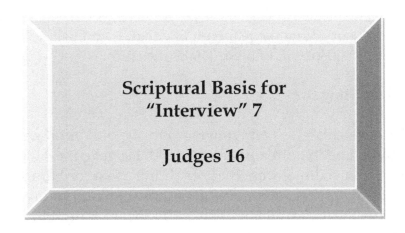

Scriptural Basis for "Interview" 7

Judges 16

"Interview" 8
Gideon

It wasn't like my faith was perfect. I played the 'show me' game pretty extensively.

The 'show me' game?

God commanded me to do something, and I responded by asking him to prove that I had heard him correctly. That whole 'laying out a fleece' thing that has become so popular over the years... that was mine.

And what was God's response?

He allowed it. I'm not sure why. He certainly didn't owe me an explanation. And he doesn't always give signs as evidence. I guess he knew I needed it.

Knew you needed proof?

Yes. Although in my own defense, it's not as though God was asking me to trust him with a few minor details in my daily life. It was life itself, as well as the lives of all the soldiers under my command. He asked me for everything all at once.

And you weren't sure about letting him have it all.

Are you?

...

Yeah, that's how I felt too. So God provided multiple signs to reassure me and build my confidence.

What kinds of signs?

There was the fleece test of course - and he allowed that twice. Then there were the irrational instructions to intentionally thin the troops when we were already vastly outnumbered - not the sign I would have chosen, but one that definitely put the responsibility on Him! And finally there were the two Midianites in their own tent – these are enemy combatants mind you – where one interpreted the other's dream, mentioning me by name and foretelling *our* victory. That one really got me!

These signs made a difference?
They did. You don't take three hundred men into battle against hundreds of thousands unless you are sure about the one sending you in. And God bolstered my faith through these signs enough for me to follow him.

What do you think you would have done if God had not provided so many signs?

I don't know. Our hearts can waver, especially when everything is on the line. I received so much courage each time I heard from the Lord... I'm not sure I would have led the army into battle without his reassurances.

One last question... this is the one I've been dying to ask. What about people who never get to see those kinds of signs? Those who listen with all their hearts and are met with only silence? Or what about people like me who search for signs under every rock, always trying to discover the right path? What about us?

I'm going to be completely vulnerable for a moment... Signs are for babies.

What?

Don't get me wrong. They are a gift. And they are valuable. But signs are mainly to encourage us when our faith is weak, not strong. We ask for proof because we do not fully trust that God's heart toward us is good. In that way, signs are for babies. Not that we can't ask. Not that He won't meet us in that way. And not that we can't receive and appreciate them. But it is God's deep desire that we eventually grow past that.

Past the need for reassurance?

Past the need for proof. To love the God who loved us first... this is why we are here, and few things glorify God as much as when we walk by faith, trusting in who he is, especially when we are not allowed to see more than what is normal.

Like what Christ says to Thomas...

Yes. Blessed are those who have NOT seen, and yet have believed. In this way, you are capable of a greater faith. I asked for proof, and God provided it. But there is a deeper, more mature faith, one that actually trusts his heart *without* requiring proof after proof. This kind of faith testifies to the trustworthiness of God. It declares that God's heart is good! I must admit, I am a bit jealous of that opportunity and of your place in the story. Seeing that invitation, knowing that God wants to grow people into men and women of faith and freedom and power? Makes me wish I had spent more time asking for faith than for signs...

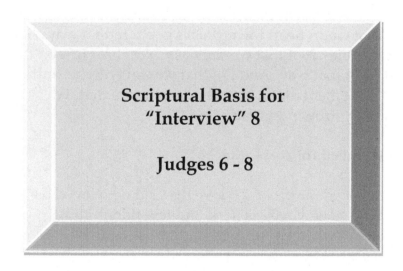

Scriptural Basis for
"Interview" 8

Judges 6 - 8

"Interview" 9
Enoch

So is it true that you never died?

Wow. Just jump right to it, huh?

It is kind of the highlight of your story.

Still, that's a very personal thing to ask someone right off the line. What if the tables were turned? What if I walked into your office, we exchanged names, and I immediately asked how your life ended?

I see... you're right. Sorry. Would you like a cup of coffee?

No, I was just giving you a hard time... I never died! How cool is that!

I've always been curious - what was it like? I mean, how did it happen? Was it all smoke and thunder and chariots of fire or did you just fade out? Was there a door? A cloud? A stairway?

Here's the thing... I don't mind talking about it, but people get so focused on that one part of my story that they completely miss the bigger part.

The bigger part?

See, that's what I mean. Everyone is so fascinated with the ending that they ignore the fact that I actually had a very long life. In terms of time invested, that was a much bigger part of the story.

Really? I've never heard that part.

Sure you have. You just skimmed over it.

It says God 'took you away.'

Before that.

What, the part that says you 'walked faithfully with God'?

Yes. That part. I walked with God, and I walked with him here for a really, really long time. I made it to three hundred and sixty five!

Three hundred and sixty five? That's one year. No offense, Enoch, but I know people who have walked with God a lot longer than that.

No, not three hundred and sixty-five days. Three hundred and sixty-five years! You're looking at me like I've lost my mind, but I'm not lying to you. Things were different before the Flood.

The Flood? As in the 'Noah and the ark' flood?

That's the one. Noah was my great grandson, and people before him lived a very long time.

Like more than three centuries?

Like a lot more. My son lived over nine. Most people did. It wasn't uncommon.

So people just kept living, all old and crippled for hundreds of years? That seems cruel.

No, we weren't old and crippled. Like I said, things were very different before the flood changed the earth. A hundred years was considered young, and men were in their prime for centuries after that.

In their prime for centuries?

How else do you think Noah was able to build the ark? He was over 500 when he started, and that's not the kind of project a person could take on if they were frail and used up.

I suppose. So hundreds of years...

And healthy and strong for almost all of it.

I can't imagine how much you could learn and build if you had hundreds of years to live, all of it at your best.

It's true. We came a long way in a short time. Cities sprang up. Technology raced forward. We were truly ruling over the earth and subduing it, just as God had charged us to do in the beginning.

That sounds exciting.

In some ways it was. But it was also terrifying. Men were powerful and aggressive, and wickedness was increasing as rapidly as everything else. We grew in numbers and wealth and strength, but we also grew in evil.

But you walked with God.

I was the exception. That's why it got written down. If everyone was walking with God, it wouldn't have stood out enough to be noticed. The reality is that most people walked away. They were building cities and taking land and seizing power. They worshipped gods of their own invention. They made deals with demons. They lied. They shed innocent blood. They invented new ways of doing evil. They forgot love. They forgot God. For centuries I watched them fall away. The world became a very dark, ugly place. That's why He destroyed it. That's why He sent the flood.

But you weren't there for that. You had already been 'taken away.'

That's right.

And what was that like – to be taken away?

You're really locked in on that question.

It's the one everyone wants to know.

Fair enough. Like I said, I had been walking with God for a long, long time.

And then?

Then we took another step.

That's it? Just another step?

Just another step. He took me away and the walk went on. We've been walking ever since.

Wait, you're still walking with God?

Oh yes! It's fantastic!

But... where are you going?

Everywhere.

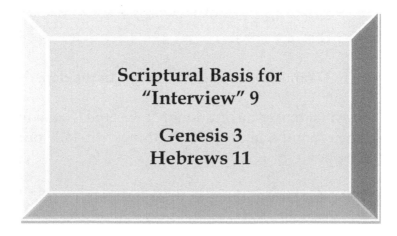

Scriptural Basis for "Interview" 9

Genesis 3
Hebrews 11

"Interview" 10
Daniel

I am glad it worked out for you to meet me here. I think it's the perfect setting for this interview.

How could I resist? When you described this place, I knew I had to see it for myself. What did you call it again?

A zoo.

Yes. A zoo. Fantastic! What will we get to see?

We'll start with the lions. A lion is a really big cat.

I'm familiar.

Do they frighten you?

Of course. They are lions!

But you're Daniel. You survived a night in the den.

You think that makes me immune? It was the Lord who closed their mouths, not me. Those things will kill you. I've seen it happen.

They look so peaceful there in their habitat.

Without the walls and moats between us – if we were to stumble upon them out in an open field somewhere – I guarantee that 'peaceful' is not how you would describe them. You would forget the beauty and grace and majesty you ascribe to them now. In fact, you would forget everything except trying to escape with your life.

There are men who have tamed them.

That may be. Man tames many things. But one day the walls and bars will come down, and those things man thinks he has mastered will turn and devour him.

Are you still talking about lions?

No.

I didn't think so. What would you like to see next?

You have the map there. What does it say?

It shows us right here, passing between the lion and the eagle. After that, we see the bear during feeding time. The leopard enclosure and the aviary are next, followed by a truly fearsome beast.

I am not sure we should venture past that.

Very well. We can turn off to a different trail that will lead us to the ram, then the goat.

Really... What else?

There is a large statue in the center of the park. Would you like me to describe it to you?

No need. I saw it when it was still under construction. What I am curious about is whether or not you have witnessed the appearance of the rock that destroys the statue?

As a matter of fact, we have.

Did it change the world?

More than you can imagine.

Then the kingdom is here?! You are living in the presence of the Son of Man?

He has come, and will come again. We are almost there...

What about the kingdoms of men? What of Babylon, Persia, Greece, and Rome?

All came and went, just as you were shown. Jerusalem was rebuilt, then destroyed, then built again. And all the prophecies about the Messiah were fulfilled.

It is like something out of a dream!
Yes, especially one of yours.

I must ask... What was his name?

The Messiah?

Yes. What did they call him?

Don't you know? He is called Immanuel. Yeshua is his name. He is the Root of David, the Son of Man, the Lamb of God... and the Lion of Judah!

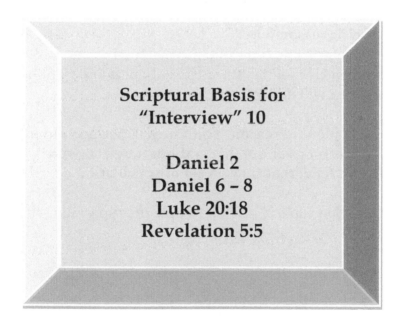

**Scriptural Basis for
"Interview" 10**

**Daniel 2
Daniel 6 – 8
Luke 20:18
Revelation 5:5**

"Interview" 11
Well Woman

Good morning. Or... I suppose it's closer to noon, isn't it?

Yes. I chose this time on purpose.

Any specific reason why?

This is when He met me. It was just about noon, right here at this well. I will never forget.

Ah, I see. Splendid reason. You know, there are a lot of inferred teachings about that – about why you were drawing water at that time. A lot of speculation...

Of course. Speculation is what people do, especially with outsiders.

You were an outsider?

To the Jews, yes. They have no love for Samaritans. There is a lot of bad blood there.

Why the division? Weren't you all Israelites? Didn't you all literally come from the same family?

It's complicated. After the reign of Solomon, the people of Israel fractured, our family tribes splitting into two separate kingdoms. Jerusalem remained the capital of Judah in the south, while Samaria became the capital of northern Israel.

What caused the split?

On the surface it was just people being people. Opposing views. Social tension. Politics. But underneath, something else was breeding division... idolatry. It is poisonous. The worship of other gods shattered the covenant between God and Israel, and within a single generation we became a bitterly divided kingdom with different kings and separate temples. Civil war followed, deepening the rift between the tribes, and northern Israel eventually fell to foreign invaders from Assyria. Those who survived were taken into captivity, and some intermarried with the Assyrians – a practice strictly forbidden in the Law of Moses. So even after we returned from exile there was no reconciliation. In the eyes of the tribe of Judah we Samaritans were unfaithful, tainted Gentile half-breeds.

The division was permanent? You stayed separate?

Kind of sad, huh? They wouldn't even speak to us.

Until the Messiah...

Yes. Until Jesus. It shocked me. A Jewish man speaking directly to a Samaritan woman? It was unheard of. It never happened. They normally wouldn't even see us.

So when he spoke to you it caught you off guard...

It certainly did. But only for a moment. I had all my defenses firmly in place. I wasn't about to let him corner me. I knew my theology. I knew my history. I threw it all at him.

I take it that didn't work?

He kept coming back to the one place I could not defend.

What was that?

My heart.

Your heart...

I don't know how else to explain it to you, other than to say that He saw me. He really, truly saw me. Do you know how rare that is? It's crazy... we all have these eyes that we look around with all day, but we almost never stop and truly see each other.

Isn't that something?

It's as if there is a whole layer of sight that isn't physical – a deeper and more personal level of seeing – but we live most of our lives with it turned off.

Wait – you had multiple husbands. Are you telling me that none of them saw you?

Maybe one did. Perhaps two took the time. But it wasn't often. It certainly wasn't normal. I must admit, part of that was my fault. I didn't usually let them see too much.

You kept them at a distance?

It's safer that way. They can't reject you if they can't really see you. Most people figure that out pretty fast, and we learn to hide ourselves, only letting people get glimpses of the parts we think they'll like.

Wow. That's pretty convicting, actually.

It's tragic. And common. You end up being invisible. Or at least unknown.

Or out at the well at noon by yourself.

Yes. All by yourself. Until one day someone is there waiting for you.

But not just anyone.

No. Not just anyone.

The Messiah. Waiting just for you.

Amazing, isn't it! He wasn't there by accident. Yeshua came looking for people like me. There is this other woman – her name is Hagar – she would tell you the same thing. You should talk to her sometime… fascinating story. She met the LORD near a spring that would become a well

51

much like this one. After that encounter, she gave this name to the LORD: 'You are the God who sees me.'

That sounds awfully familiar. You know this woman?

Only in spirit. She lived a long time ago. Before Jews and Samaritans. Before Israel.

But she had the same experience as you?

I think she did. She was alone, rejected, lost in life, and God saw her. That is what God does. He sees us. The real us. Samaritan? Adulterer? Outcast? He saw right through all of that. Through my theology. Through my history. Through my arguments and defenses to the heart he loved when he knit me together. He told me everything I ever did and saw the real me through it all.

And who do you think he saw?

Oh I know who he saw... His.

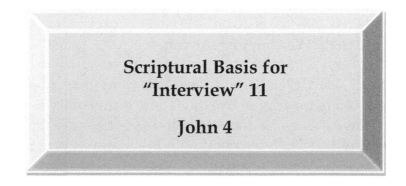

Scriptural Basis for "Interview" 11

John 4

"Interview" 12
John the Apostle

Welcome, John. Great to have you. Big fan of your books.

Thanks. I get a lot of mixed reviews.

I bet you do. You offer an insider's perspective, though, and a lot of us are profoundly grateful for that.

Each different account plays a part. I loved being allowed to contribute a piece of the puzzle.

You're being modest. You contributed more than one. Speaking of which, I've got a perplexing question to ask about something you wrote.

Let me guess... is it about Revelation?

No. I have my own theories about Revelation.

Oh boy... you and everyone else.

Don't worry, it's nothing specific. I'm not trying to identify the antichrist or pinpoint the date of Armageddon.

That's refreshing.

My take on all that - based on how other things unfolded in scripture – is that while every promise will be perfectly fulfilled, all of it crystal clear looking back, most things will happen right under our noses.

That's much better than what I thought you might say.

Take the rapture for instance...

Oh, you were doing so well. Don't ruin it with more words.

I just think it might happen in a way that is so natural that people won't even realize what it is.

Perhaps. I guess we'll see.

Or will we?

Right. So what was the perplexing question you were going to ask?

Oh yes! Why does the Bible say that you are 'the disciple that Jesus loved'? Didn't Jesus love all of you? Why the distinction? Did he not love the others, or were you just his favorite?

Where in the Bible does it refer to me as 'the disciple that Jesus loved'?

In the Gospel according to John.

According to who?

John.

Interesting… who do you think wrote that?

Well, you, obviously.

Right. That Gospel is my personal eye-witness account of Jesus' life and ministry. And in that account I refer to myself as 'the disciple that Jesus loved'… because that is my testimony! It is not a statement about the love Jesus had for anyone else. It is a declaration of one very specific, crucial fact: he loved me! That is the reality that I lived.

So you call yourself 'the disciple that Jesus loved' because that is central to your story?

It is! In my story, one of the most important truths I get to communicate is that Jesus truly loves me. Not exclusively, but personally. Faithful, all-in, endless love. Hopefully, in your own story you are declaring the same thing.

My story... so if I write a book I should put myself in it and call that character 'the one Jesus loves'?

No – your real story! Your actual life, day in and day out, with all of your thoughts and actions and everything else, should be resounding with the truth that 'I am the one Jesus loves.' Not merely 'a one'. THE one! If you want the world to know that truth, you've got to live it out.

That's why you describe yourself that way in your Gospel?

Yes. Because it's true. I claim it. I am the disciple that Jesus loves. And so are you.

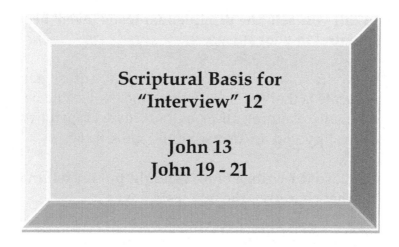

Scriptural Basis for
"Interview" 12

John 13
John 19 - 21

"Interview" 13
Zacchaeus

I thought you would be smaller.

Thanks. I think...

It's just - we've got this song about you.

'Wee little man' right? I've heard. Guess everybody is famous for something.

But you're not that small.

Dude, I'm not a smurf. It just says I was too short to see over the crowd. That's a lot of us.

Yeah. My bad. It's funny – the images that get stuck in your head.

No problem. I was stuck in some pretty foolish ideas for a long time myself.

Well, we all have our shortcomings -

Wow. Seriously?
Come on, that was a good one. In all seriousness, though, the shortcomings are real. We all have weaknesses,

failures, fears... and even when we appear to be "doing life" really well, the hard reality is that all of our earthly strength and wealth and knowledge is temporary. We ultimately lose it all.

I agree. Is there a question for me in there somewhere?

Yeah. You were a wealthy man. Not very well liked, but wealthy. One encounter with Jesus turns all that upside down. Now I realize that kind of life transformation is something that Christ tends to do, but it seems to happen really quickly in your story. I was hoping that you would be willing to share exactly what it was that brought about such a sudden shift.

I see. Quick conversion. I must have seen something, right? Something spectacular must have happened.

That's what I would like to find out. You climb the tree, Jesus calls you down to host him at your place, and the next thing you know you are giving away half of everything you own and making restitution for past swindlings. What happened? What is your explanation?

God knocks.

God knocks? Ok... you're going to have to translate that one for me.
Jesus says it himself, 'Here I am! I stand at the door and knock. If anyone hears my voice and opens the door, I will come in and eat with that person, and they with me.'

That's a pretty amazing promise.

Here's the thing... it's true. Jesus wasn't lying. He is knocking and genuinely wants to join us. I know it because I lived it.

Jesus knocked and you answered?

Yes. Quite literally. And it really was a choice. I was free to decide whether to open the door. I could have refused. I could have kept it shut. Or...

Or?

Or I could let Him in. It was that simple.

And that fast?

Well, I can't say it was fast.

From Jesus calling you out of the tree until supper that night? That sounds pretty fast to me.

Oh, the moment of opening the door and being set free was fast. No doubt about that. But God had been knocking for a long time.

Since when?
Basically my whole life. For years I ignored it. I was busy. I had things to do. Money to make. But he kept knocking, and eventually I realized that I had to know who was there.

That is why I went to see Jesus. That is why I climbed the tree.

That is why you opened the door...

Yes. I am eternally thankful for that, and so grateful that He never stopped knocking.

Oh, me too! I'd be in bad shape if he knocked once and walked away.

But that's not who he is.

No it's not. So he knocked and knocked and knocked, and you finally answered and let him in. What happened then?

Best supper I've ever had...

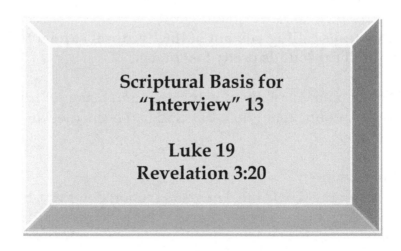

Scriptural Basis for "Interview" 13

**Luke 19
Revelation 3:20**

"Interview" 14
Mary

When did you first realize that Jesus was different?

I would have to say it was before he was born.

That early?

Well, when the reveal party is hosted by an angel...

Fair point. You did have advance notice. What about Jesus himself? What was the first thing he did that made him seem... other?

I was actually still carrying him. He wasn't even showing yet. I went to visit my relative Elizabeth, who was also pregnant, and as I greeted her the baby in her belly responded dramatically to the baby in mine. That's the first time I saw a hint of his effect on others. Elizabeth and I didn't fully realize the significance of the relationship our two boys would have, but in that moment there was no doubt that God was involved. The presence of the Holy Spirit filled the room, and we shared a tiny glimpse of the hope that was on the way.

People were being moved even before he was born?

That's who he was. Announced by angels, worshipped by the wise, loved by the weak and the poor, and hated by the prideful. He had an effect on everyone. Long before he officially began his ministry, he was already moving hearts.

I've never thought about that before – how Jesus interacted with people in Nazareth for quite a few years while simply going about his day to day routine. It is hard to picture him just doing regular life, but I suppose he did?

Yes. We had him with us until he was thirty. Three decades of our family being together.

I must admit, I'm intrigued at the thought of him quietly ministering to people during that time. How fascinating! Now at some point, he puts down the carpenter's hammer and begins doing some dramatically different things. Take us back to the wedding at Cana.

Ah yes, the wedding. Such a special day.

According to the Biblical accounts, it seems you may have provided a little push to get the ball rolling in terms of the miraculous signs that Jesus revealed. How did you even know that he would be able to help with the wine?

Ah, a valid question! Because he hadn't done any miracles yet, right?

We have his whole story here in front of us - all the amazing wonders - but the wedding at Cana was the first.

Before that he was apparently so normal that even his own brothers did not know who he was. So if he hadn't yet done anything like that, how did you think to ask him?

There are things a mother just knows. He was my son. I carried him. I nursed him. I raised him. There was so much stored up in my heart, so many things that I had pondered through the years. I knew heaven was in there. I just didn't know when it would break out.

Why did you choose that particular time to ask? I am sure there were other moments, other hard seasons before that when a little divine provision would have really helped you and Joseph out. Why ask here? Why now? Was there a personal debt involved? Were you stirred by a prompting by God's Spirit? What was it about this wedding?

It was just... right.

But Jesus said that his time had not yet come...

It was not yet time for his wedding! That is most certainly true. His marriage celebration is still approaching. But looking back, there is no doubt that it was the right miracle to start with.

What makes you say that?

Because God deals in beauty. Even as he works to meet our needs, drawing life into the world like water from a well, he does the drawing as an artist! Look closely and you will see that the water and the wine are knit together from the beginning. The Flood and the Red Sea, Passover and Baptism, Melchizedek and Moses. Soak in the poem God is writing and you will see that the water and the wine are there throughout. Then overlay that with the realization that the heart of Jesus' mission is reconciliation – a restoration of love if you will – and that his beautiful work culminates in the reuniting of God and man at the wedding feast of the Lamb. Soon it all starts to reveal something very intentional. Water and wine and weddings. They are woven into the story from start to finish. In light of these things, what more beautiful way could there be for Jesus to begin his work?

You could see all that ahead of time?

Oh no! Not at all. But a mother's heart is a mysterious thing. Sometimes we do the right thing without knowing it just by loving our babies!

That's a nice way to put it. So you asked Jesus to help, then instructed the servers to do whatever he said. What were you expecting? What did you think was going to happen?

I didn't know. But I had no doubt he could provide what was needed.

And the water became wine.

Yes.

And three years later, the wine became blood.

Yes...

You were told that a sword would pierce your own soul.

Yes. And it did.

When did that happen? Was it when they took him?

I do not speak of that. He accomplished the mission God assigned him. That is all that matters. But a mother does not speak of what they did to my son. To watch it was enough.

You saw the crucifixion...?

This is what I saw: The water became wine. The wine became blood. And his blood was poured out to purify the bride.

What a beautiful gift! Oh, are you leaving? I'm sorry. I didn't mean to upset you.

Upset? No, I'm not upset. Just excited. You'll have to excuse me, though. There is a lot to do and not much time left.

Are you getting ready for something?

Of course. Haven't you heard? There is another wedding to prepare for. My son is getting married!

Your son... Married? When?

Soon!

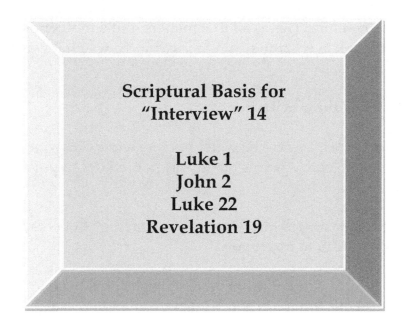

**Scriptural Basis for
"Interview" 14**

**Luke 1
John 2
Luke 22
Revelation 19**

"Interview" 15
Benaiah

The most recent interview went really well.

Yeah?

Well, I thought it did anyway. We had a remarkable guest.

Who?

Oh, just someone named Mary.

Mary... Which Mary? You're not talking about the mother of the Messiah!

That's the one!

What? How am I supposed to follow that?

You'll do fine. Besides, if she was still here she wouldn't let you worry about it for a second.

Immaculate grace?

Radiant with it.

As expected.

And so we come to you.

From one extreme to the other.

Oh, I wouldn't go that far. Nobility, courage, valor... these have their own measure of grace.

Perhaps.

Would you care to say more about that?

No.

Has anyone ever accused you of being overly wordy?

Also no.

Well, you are a man of action. I suppose it fits. Though it is going to make it difficult to interview you.

Ask better questions.

Very well. Why do you chase lions into pits?

Same reason everybody else does.

... Ok, that gives me nothing.

It was a silly question. Do better.

Umm... in David's army, how do you get to be one of the Mighty Men? Is it kill count? A test of strength? Some kind of quest? Is there an application form? Does David decide who makes it, or is it more of a consensus/vote among the troops type of thing?

Insider information.

That's why I am asking you. You're an insider.

You're not.

Wow. You are not making this easy. Let me try one more... you didn't take part in any of the coups and rebellions against David. Why not?

Loyalty.

But rebelling at the right time could have drastically improved your position.

Loyalty.

A lot of military leaders took that route...

Loyalty.

I see. Is that how you ended up in charge of the entire army?

Possibly.

So loyalty... would you say that is at the heart of how you carry yourself?

It's a big deal.

Alright. That's about all I've got for you. This tooth extraction is just about over. Anything else you would like to leave the reader with?

If you look into my story, you're not going to find me saying a whole lot. I just got it done. Sometimes words are valuable. In times of testing and hardship and battle, however, you eventually just have to shut up, strap on your sword, and take the field. See you out there.

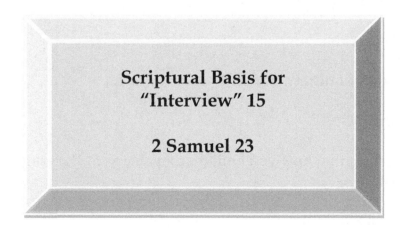

Scriptural Basis for "Interview" 15

2 Samuel 23

"Interviews" 16
Goliath of Gath

Come on in. Watch your head.

Oh… a curse on your low ceilings!

Sorry about that. I had planned to have our meeting outside until this storm rolled in. Here, please have a seat. How tall are you anyway?

Nine feet nine inches.

Nine-nine! Wow. There probably aren't a whole lot of houses where you can stand up straight.

No. Not many. My house, though – my house had grand ceilings! Like a king's palace!

I'm sure it was magnificent. I'd like to offer you some refreshments. Are you hungry?

Always.

What is your favorite thing to eat?

Yes.

Hey! Did you just make a joke?

This surprises you?

To be honest, it kind of does. A sense of humor is not something I associate with the name Goliath.

Because I am a big mean monster, right?

Well...

I'm a person, ok? Big, yes. Flawed, sure. But I am a lot more like you than you might think.

I'm starting to get a glimpse of that, though it will probably take me a while to reconfigure the image of you in my mind. Perhaps it will help if you tell me – what is a common misconception that people have about you?

That I am a bully.

You did fight a boy half your size.

That wasn't my doing! I made my challenge to the entire army of Israel. I expected to face off in deadly combat against their mightiest and bravest warrior. I expected them to send their best, their strongest, their most dangerous. I had no idea they would send a boy.

You know... you're right. You didn't choose David.

No.

72

But God did.

And that is where I was in the wrong. I was not wrong in fighting for my nation, but I was wrong for fighting against the God of Israel. I did not realize who He was.

Say more about that.

I bowed to the gods of the Philistines in order to receive good fortune and victory over my enemies. I did not realize that those gods were not gods at all. I did not understand that the God who created life itself – the God who owns the heavens and the earth, the true and living God - had chosen little Israel as his set apart possession.

I see. So when you defied the armies of Israel...

I defied the armies of God. And when that little boy raced across the field to fight me, it was not a little boy that I met.

It was the LORD.

It was. It was God Almighty. My maker and yours. And there is no shield wide enough, no spear long enough, no sword sharp enough for a man to stand against that God.

Not even a man who is ten feet tall?

Size and strength - what are they to the God who hands them out? Is God threatened by anything man can do?

How do you reach him? What weapons can touch him? How do you grapple with God?

I don't know.

No man ever caused me to turn and flee. I was a champion! You would not want to meet me on the battlefield or see me charge in your direction. But God does not tremble at the approach of men. He has only to remove his breath and we fall. Who can fight that?

Many try.

Fools, all of us. We rally to banners and causes. We race out onto the field, roaring our boasts and challenges. But in the end it all blows off like smoke. When the battle is over and our borrowed strength is stripped away, only one allegiance remains.

What allegiance is that?

The allegiance your heart declares when you stand before the LORD. This is what matters. Were you aligned with him or against him? There is no middle ground.

You chose a side, didn't you?

I chose wrong. I lined up against the LORD and my strength was exposed as weakness. I took my stand against God himself, and a child cut me down.

Thank you for that testimony, and for coming in today. It was actually really good to hear from you. Before you head back out into the storm, I'd like to offer you the last word. If Goliath could give the world of men one parting piece of wisdom, what would it be?

Learn from the fallen giants…
There is one God, and you are not Him.

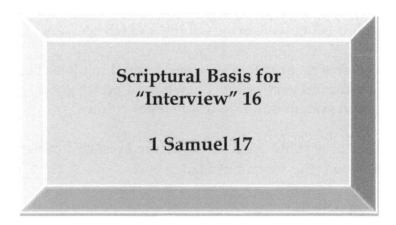

Scriptural Basis for
"Interview" 16

1 Samuel 17

"Interview" 17

Gehazi

Kind of barren out here...

It's just the dry season. A little rain and things will green back up.

Mmmm... no, there's something else. It feels barren in a deeper kind of way.

Oh, that goes without saying. Leper colonies aren't exactly known for being wellsprings of life and effervescence.

Effervescence... now there's a word you don't hear being thrown around very often. They have a pretty good education system out here in the leper colony?

No. But I wasn't always a leper. Before I picked up the disease I was the servant of Elisha.

The prophet?

Yes. He had started out as the servant of Elijah, and when he succeeded his master, I stepped into the servant's role.

That's a pretty impressive spiritual pedigree you've got there. Elijah... Elisha... then you... But we don't hear much about the great prophet Gehazi.

You don't have to remind me. I live with that. There is far greater suffering for me there than from the leprosy.

What happened?

The short version? I talked myself into destroying myself.

Details, please. Plenty of people destroy themselves. What makes your story significant?

It's embarrassing to talk about, especially given the spiritual lineage you mentioned. When the sky is the limit the ground hits pretty hard. Let's just say that I chose a path that culminated in some extremely foolish decisions.

What was that path? Where did you steer wrong? Were there warning signs?

Warning signs? Sure. When you find yourself lying to make things happen, or making moves that require you to push God off to the side in order to advance yourself – that is the road. It doesn't lead anywhere good.

Did you know you were on that road? Did you understand that you were heading toward destruction?

Deep down I did. We all have that still small voice that calls to our hearts, but with enough practice we can get terribly good at ignoring it.

Been there. Done that. Paid the price.

That's the thing - there is a very real price. We can squeeze our eyes shut and clamp our hands over our ears, but that voice isn't calling out for no reason.

That has to be agonizing for God.

I can't imagine what He feels, calling out to us, trying to bring us back from the ledge, watching us inch closer and closer to death. But we love the ledge. We sneak out there, smothering his calls with shouts about what we deserve.

Now those are some loud voices!

Oh, we love them don't we? We love to hear how much we deserve. That's how people sell us things. We put those voices on a loop in our minds until we convince ourselves that we should have what we 'deserve' right now. That's what happened to me.

I feel like I've chased those voices quite a few times.

It's easy. They taste so sweet. That is what I meant when I said I talked myself into my own destruction. I followed those lies right to the place where they stole all I had.

You lost it all?

It could have been Elijah, Elisha, and Gehazi.
Instead it is Elijah, Elisha, and the foolish fallen leper.

That's a tragic ending. I know we can benefit from your warning, but what about you? Is there any hope for you?

There are rumors of One who is not afraid to touch lepers. One who can even reach those who have gone over the ledge. I hope to meet him someday. That is one voice I can't wait to hear.

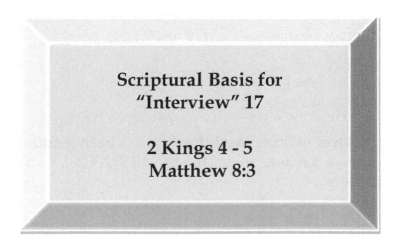

Scriptural Basis for "Interview" 17

2 Kings 4 - 5
Matthew 8:3

"Interview" 18
Legion

yes, closer, come
linger here with us
such a pretty pretty house
name the itch and we will scratch
simple keys is all we ask
make us just a little room
such saucy rent we offer

This house is claimed.

ah! we see it now
He lives here
His house, ah!
tear the flesh from this one
quick! before he speaks

You will tear nothing. An interview has been granted. In the name of Yeshua, Son of the Most High God, stand and answer.

OWWW!
let us go!
let us go!
please let us go!

I will not.

no room to breathe, too hot
throat clamped tight with ire and spite
outside is worse
dry, too dry
no rest, we fly, we search the tombs
find the dead still walking
pretty house at last
unguarded door and open wide
rush from west and south and east
hurry, enter, bind him quick
draw him into shadow
cut the root

What have you done to him?

his house no more
keys so easily surrendered
Hostage ours, by self enslaved
sits and scribbles on the walls
drool-soaked beard, piss-stained pants
a mockery of what he was

It's awful. You have buried him alive.

fallen from the heights
that horrid path we know too well
failure in his father's eyes
his mother cries 'disgrace!'
behold the wretched captive man
pretty pretty house

Who is it? Who is the man you have you enslaved?

why ask that?
he is no one
nor can he recall
busy now, he toils for us
amazing what they'll do
pretty house, pretty pretty house
crowded though
too many mouths to feed

What is his name?

Worthless
Lost
Damned
Alone
we call him all these things

And your name?

you've heard our name already
we are many
an army to ourselves

I have heard your name. And I know the One who made you flee. Tell me, when He approached, how did you know it was Him?

An absurd question! Why should we tell you that?

**The interview has been granted. By the authority of the
Risen Christ, I charge you - tell the truth!**

we were among the tombs
all was dark, no trace of light
then the darkness fled
His face... we know His face!
from ancient times
chains fall open
keys torn from our hands
pretty house goes free

He forced you out. He took back what is His.

a million crooked fingers
stab in all directions
silence fools! you lost my house!
my house, you mean!
no, mine!
i'll skin you all alive
you are a weakling! gnaw your tongue!
mock on, mock on! all hope is gone
the abyss opens its mouth
oh no!
please, let us find another house
any house will do

**You are trembling. Every one of you quakes and stares.
What shook you then shakes you now. You melt like wax.
There is no place for you to turn, no escape from the
terror of the truth. You will see Him again, and soon.**

it is established from of old
steel band around our days
account for evil wicked ways
balance due on His return
for every blood-stained debt unpaid
stripped of power, stripped of strength
fire like a lake awaits
when next we see His face

**You collapse in heaps like ashes. The softest breeze could
drive you off. After ages of torment and oppression, you
have become nothing. I see your eyes cloud over. It comes
for you... suffering far deeper than any man has known.
Despite my loathing of you and my rage at all the harm
you've done, I cannot help but feel a stab of pity. I see
now why the Lord let you flee - the great mercy that
comes from above. But there is no swine herd here today.
Tell me, what will you do now?**

we will tear at you
with all we have
until we are no more
steal
kill
destroy
this is what we've chosen
this is who we are
so let us in and hate yourself
camp within our lies
carve you from the inside out
despised birthright sold for soup
lonely broken bondage
our hate-filled gift to you

last attack on the face of God
burn the pretty pretty houses
til some of you are here with us
your screams joined to ours

That's enough! Silence now. I am claimed, and far beyond your reach. His grip is stronger than yours. So go and wait in the Abyss, for your time is almost over. The fire is made ready and the Son is on his way.

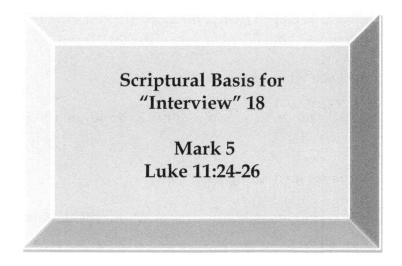

Scriptural Basis for "Interview" 18

Mark 5
Luke 11:24-26

"Interview" 19
Esther

Your name means star...

That's true.

It suits you.

Do you say that for my benefit or for yours?

What do you mean?

Compliments can be many things. Too often they are not compliments at all.

I'm not sure what to say.

Be honest. Did you compliment me to build me up or to serve yourself?

You have seen right through me.

Then let us begin again, this time without the flattery.

As you wish.

You asked about my name. It is Esther, yes, but it was originally Hadassah.

Hadassah... What does that mean?

It means myrtle in the language of the Jews.

Then where does Esther come from?

Esther is the name I am called among the Persians.

You are a Persian then?

It is hard to say no, as I became Queen of Persia, but I have always been a Jew.

Jew... like the religion?

Like the family. When I say that I am a Jew, I mean that I am an Israelite from the tribe, or family, of a man named Judah.

A man named Judah was your ancestor?

Correct. Our entire Israelite tribe is descended from him.

And Israelite means?

Israelite means 'of Israel.' Israel was Judah's father. These names reveal where I come from – my lineage. I am a direct descendant of Abraham, then Isaac, then Jacob (who God renamed Israel) and then Israel's son Judah. This makes me 'of Judah' - a Jew.

Got it. But you were a Jew living in Persia?

That's right. The tribe of Judah was conquered by the Babylonians and its people exiled, taken far from our homeland, far from the land of Israel.

I see. And as a Jew in Persia, you had two names. One Hebrew. One Persian.

Exactly.

Which do you prefer?

Which name?

Yes. Which of your names do you like best?

Oh, I adore them both. One is like the distant call of Jerusalem, beckoning to my heart with the sweet voice of my people. The other reminds me of the call God placed on my life here, for as a star is a light in the darkness, so the LORD's purpose for me was to bring a light into a very dark time in the history of Israel.

I must admit, there is more to you than I expected.

More flattery?

No. This is sincere. I'd heard about the beauty pageant that led you to the throne, so I expected pretty. I didn't expect poise, balance, and self-assurance. You truly have the bearing of a queen.

Hard roads can do that. If we persevere in hardship, God can grow us in mighty ways.

You were Queen of Persia. The whole world was at your feet. How can you describe your road as one of hardship?

I was an orphan. My cousin adopted me after the death of my parents. And as I told you, we were exiles, all of us. Our nation was conquered and burned, its people taken by force to Babylon, which was eventually swallowed up by the Medes and Persians. There was no stability, no guaranteed safety for a group of conquered refugees. We were used and despised by many. So while I did end up in the palace, I didn't begin there. My life had its share of pain.

But God eventually led you through those hard early years into easy times later on, right?

God certainly did lead me through those hard early years, but even more desperate challenges came later. After I became queen, a prominent figure rose up in Persia who made it his mission to eradicate what was left of the Jews. He actually put an official government policy in place to have us all rounded up and murdered.

It is amazing how many times there has been a plot to destroy your people!

You are talking about our captivity in Egypt?

No. Much later... In a land you don't even know about yet there will be another, much larger and more organized attempt to destroy the Jews. Six million of you will be taken from your homes, tortured and killed.

Six million! Was that all of us?

No. In fact, one of the major outcomes of the defeat of those who tried to annihilate you is that the nation of Israel gets re-established.

We make it back to Jerusalem?!

Yes. The plan to destroy you backfired. It was the same with the Messiah.

The Messiah! He arrived at last? Then Israel is established forever! He must be seated on the throne in Jerusalem.

Well... yes and no. Foreigners killed him by hanging him on a cross.

Then he could not have been the Messiah. The Messiah will lead our people against our enemies and reign forever.

Well, he does, but only after your leaders hand him over to be executed.

Execute the Messiah! I will not believe it. We are a stiff-necked people, to be sure, but we would never...

It is what is written in the prophets. You have the words of Isaiah. Read them once more. The Messiah is the Passover Lamb. He willingly suffers and lays down his life to make atonement for the people. This was God's plan from the beginning.

You say the Messiah was killed and yet you are smiling. Why? How is there hope in any of this?

Because the grave could not hold him! The plot of the Enemy backfires! After three days in the tomb the Messiah rises to life, and by his death... he has conquered death!

Oh, I see it now! Like a flash it all becomes so clear!

What do you see?

You just told me that by his death the Messiah conquers death. The Adversary is outwitted, the ancient Accuser undone, the Enemy destroyed by his own trap. I have seen first-hand this very thing! The Adversary in my time, Haman, was the one who set in motion the attempt to exterminate the Jews, murdering us wherever we were found. But God raised me up and put me in a place where I had the ear and the heart of the king. By faith I accepted God's call for me, and by faith I shed light on Haman's plot. The king's justice came swiftly, and the Adversary died on the same gallows he had built for my family, so that what was intended to kill us actually destroyed the Enemy. The trap snapped shut on the one who built it.

It's a perfect fit. Almost as if your life was part of a greater story - a greater plan...

> A greater plan indeed! And not only for my life, but all our lives together! Death defeated. Life restored. And a risen, eternal Messiah. Praise be to God! His plan is perfect, his mercy is everlasting, and his faithfulness endures through all generations! I say it again - the plans of the LORD stand firm forever, the purposes of His heart through all generations!

No flattery intended, but you are kind of beaming right now...

What can I say? That's what Esthers do.

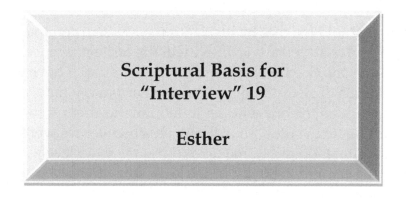

Scriptural Basis for "Interview" 19

Esther

"Interview" 20
Adam

Belly button or no?

Why is everyone so fascinated with that?

Because almost everyone else on the planet has one. The people want to know!

That's a big no on the button.

Can we get a picture for the article?

Picture of what? There's nothing there!

I know. It's crazy.

No. No picture.

Fine... We didn't really want one anyway. I was just stalling for you.

Stalling for me?

Yeah. This interview is going to be uncomfortable. I was trying to buy you a little more time.

I've done enough hiding. Ask what you need to ask.

Alright... We could talk for days about how awesome things were in Eden. And I am sure you could give us some pretty epic gardening tips. But there is basically one question that leaps out from the rest.

You want to know about the Fall...

We're not even that curious - more pissed about all the suffering and pain in the world that raced in through the door you opened. I hate to corner you, but there's no getting around this one. You ruined everything. What were you thinking, man? Seriously! You had it all.

I wanted more.

There wasn't more!

Yeah... I know.

So what happened? Was it Eve? Did she trick you?

Did Eve trick me? Oh, I see. Pin it on the woman, right? I already tried that. No. I was there with her at the tree the whole time.

The whole time?

The whole time. Eve wasn't alone with the serpent. I was with her. I heard what it said. My ears sampled the lies. For one last moment I was free. Free to choose. Free to act. Free to defend the kingdom I had been given to rule. Sword in hand, standing in the garden, easily inside the boundaries of my jurisdiction, I was well within my rights and abilities to defend us and take the thing's head off.

Wh... why didn't you?!

It said something I liked.

Which was?

It said there was more. It said I could be greater.

Greater than ruler of the earth... Wow. And what exactly did it say you had to do to become greater?

Easy. Just take it. That's all we had to do. Just claim that we were more trustworthy than God. Simple as that. Snatch the fruit of judgment. Take a bite. Be gods ourselves.

And you did.

Yeah. We did.

You are an idiot. Seriously... I am afraid there is no gentler way to frame this question, so I'm just going to say it - How could you be so stupid?

The same way you do it.

I've never...

Sure you have. Each and every time that your desires and thoughts and feelings come into direct conflict with God's living Word, you are standing there with us at that tree. And every time you decide that your heart is trustworthy and that God's heart is not, you do exactly what we did.

But...

Save the excuses, son. I know them all. God doesn't understand, right? He doesn't see? Times have changed? Come on, man. That's the same road.

No, it's not the same! We are captive now.

Oh, right. Captive. So it's not your fault that you teach each other that God's not even there? Or argue that the Bible is outdated or corrupted so that you can ignore it... Oh, how about it's 'my truth' that matters? Yeah, that's a nice spin on *exactly* what we did. Or 'I can't help it. I was made this way.' Or 'hey man, I pray to the universe.' Or 'I'm a good person.' Don't waste your time. I've heard them all. Your lies are just as broken as mine.

Hey, I don't...

Of course you do. How often are you steered entirely by your own selfish desires? How about *All. The. Time.* But that's ok, because if you feel it, it must be right. And we both know how much you like to be right! Almost as much as you like to play the hero - safely of course. Wouldn't actually want to get hurt. Or risk your savings. Or be uncomfortable for someone else. But other than that, you are down to save the world, right? Just not love the world or really serve the world. More like win the world. Some days it even looks more like conquer the world. Face it... even your compassion is tainted with self-importance.

... I – I don't ...

Yeah. I know. It's all true. In the core of your soul, you are dead and you need to be saved. You need to be remade or you are lost. And the hard part? Only God can do it. But that's tough for us, isn't it? That first tree is hard to let go. You keep running back to it, trusting yourself instead of God to do the saving.

How... how do you know all this?

Because I'm you. All of you. My name is Adam. My name is Man. And there is another tree...

**Scriptural Basis for
"Interview" 20**

Genesis 3

"Interview" 21
Jesus

I totally recognize you!

Of course you do.

You look different than the pictures.

Ha ha!

Except the laughing one. There is a little bit of you in that one.

Yeah, I like that one too.

How do you feel about that... when people try to draw you or make movies and songs about you?

Completely depends on why a person is doing it.

So it's a heart thing?

Always. Appearances can be deceiving. Words can be empty. The truth is deeper than that. The truth is in the heart. That's where I look.

What about statues and paintings? How do you feel about them?

Same thing. You have to be careful. You don't want to start worshiping the images themselves. Symbols are tricky like that. They can easily take the place of whatever they were intended to represent. It's better just to stick with me. I am here. Don't replace me with a trinket.

Replace you?

It's like staring at a picture of someone all day, completely ignoring the fact that they are sitting right there in the room with you. You don't actually look at *them*. You don't talk to them or hear what they are saying. You don't get up and go out and do life together. You just stare at their picture. Why? For good luck? For an emotional experience? It might make sense if they were gone, but I'm not gone. I'm right here, and I love you. So don't replace the real me with an image, or you will end up having a relationship with a picture and completely miss me.

That makes sense. Love you, not symbols of you. What about the other side of that – when people tear apart or destroy symbols of you? Does that hurt?

When people attack images of me or mock me in songs or movies... they are usually tearing me apart in their hearts. That is what hurts. A broken statue doesn't hurt me. Being hated by the people I created and love... that hurts.

Why don't you just get rid of those people? The world would be so much better without them.

You don't love them. That's why you can say that. But I do love them, so I can't. I still remember knitting them together. I still remember when each of their hearts began to beat. I still remember all I have in mind for them – all they could be. I still remember those first innocent moments I had with them before they were born – before the shadows stole them away. I can't forget those things.

But those things are gone. Some people just turn evil.

If it was your child, you wouldn't accept that. You wouldn't want to give up hope. There is a hard step you have to take to really give up on someone. It is a complete removal of your love. It's a lot like killing a person. I don't ever want to do that. I don't ever want to cut off one of my sons. I don't ever want to abandon one of my daughters.

But sometimes you have to?

Sometimes people choose to end us. They walk out and never come back. But I don't quit on anyone. If anyone ever turns around, I am right there.

Whew. That got heavy. Sorry. I meant to ask you about something else entirely.

I know.

Ok, let's end with a question that has perplexed men for centuries. How do you walk on water?

Haha! Walk on water? That's what has perplexed men for centuries?

Well, maybe not. But it's one of the first things I see in my head when I hear the name Jesus. I'm very visual.

Oh, I love you and your imagination! OK, visualize this... Your hands are cupped and filled with water. Do you see it?

Yeah. Sure. I can see that.

Good. Now look again down into the water in your hands and realize that you can't see the bottom.

Hey that's cool! Is this magic water?

Nope. Normal water. Except there are whales in there. Full size whales! And fish - more than you can count. The water in your hands is far too wide for you to swim across. It covers the whole earth and dances to the pull of the moon, shaping the weather and steering the wind. Can you see it? All the oceans of the world? Can you feel how much water that is?

No. It's too big. I can generalize a little bit, but I can't truly comprehend it. There's too much to wrap my brain around.

Now open your hands, and as you let it rain down upon the earth, realize that every drop of that water – all that is in it and all that it does – is mine. I made it. I established the laws and properties and boundaries that hold it in place. I divided it and put it in motion. I sustain it. I rule it. I know every wave and I schedule each tide and I keep the whole living thing going every second of every day. So walking on it? Yeah, not a problem.

I see it! So beautiful... It really is alive, isn't it!

It sure is. Yet even the oceans are not as full of life as you. You are made in my image. You are priceless to me. And I want to do life with you. So how about it... feel like walking on water?

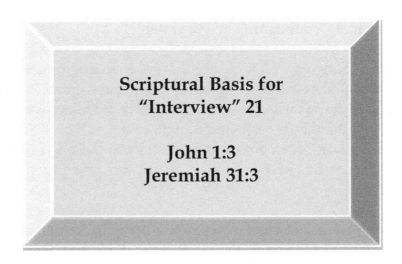

Scriptural Basis for "Interview" 21

**John 1:3
Jeremiah 31:3**

"Interview" 22
Satan

What makes you qualified to conduct these interviews?
Putting your words in other people's mouths... it is the
height of presumption!

Glad you could make it. I'm sure you are busy.

Don't think for a moment that I am going to answer your
questions if you refuse to answer mine.

**Oh, did you ask a question? I must have mistaken it for
an accusation. That's what you do, right?**

Clever. Clever and impudent. I like that. But yes, I did ask
a question. How are you qualified to do what you are
doing? You aren't, which is why you tried to dodge the
issue, but I will not allow your arrogance to go unchecked!
You are a fraud, dealing fast and loose with scripture.

Trespassing on your turf?

Watch yourself. I can expose you in a heartbeat! Or do you
think people will be uninterested to learn how you have
disqualified yourself over and over again? I could begin by
listing your moral failures right now. Would you like them

chronological or alphabetical? I know, let's start with the most innocent ones and work our way up to the worst.

Yes, by all means. List each and every sin that Christ has not paid for.

That's not -

Your jurisdiction ends at the cross! Any charge against me that God has not forgiven you are free to declare publicly. Please proceed.

...

No? Very well. Then it's my turn to ask a question. Do you have the ability to tell the truth?

Truth is relative. Didn't they teach you anything in school?

Interesting... unable to speak the truth. What about creation? Do you have the ability to create?

Of course. I create many things. The world is full of my influence.

Like what? What is one thing that you brought into existence from nothing? Was it the grass? The sky? The stars? Which was you?

...

Nothing? I see... so you can't actually create. You can only steal and twist what God has already created. Noted. What about love? Can you love?

I can do whatever I want. 'Do what though wilt' is the whole of the law!

Oh... So it's not that you can't love, you just don't want to, is that it?

Of course. Love is insipid.

Got it. So you are unable to speak the truth, unable to create, and unable to love. What exactly can you do?

I can end you!

Can you though? I feel like you would have – I mean – if you could.

Ten out of ten people die. That's a one hundred percent success rate. And you are very much in line.

What percentage of those deaths are permanent?

...

That's the big secret, isn't it? The one you try to keep hidden? I know you are a skilled liar, but I'm beginning to suspect that death is not as big a deal as you make it out to be.

That's brave talk, but courage falters when the moment draws near. No one wins when it comes to death.

Aren't you forgetting someone? You and I both know that there is one who willingly laid down his life and ripped the keys of death and hell right out of your hand before he rose again. Or were you not counting Him?

Lies. All lies.

If it was a lie, wouldn't you be the one saying it?

...

I'm curious - are you at least honest with yourself? Do you creep off once in a while and face the truth of how very little time you have left?

I can cause worlds of pain with the time I have left.

What sweet irony! The more pain you inflict, the more God redeems. How brilliant is that! You cannot help but attack and destroy, but the more damage you do, the more God heals and restores in ways that are even deeper than what was there to start with. You are actually enriching Heaven! You are adding to God's glory in spite of yourself.

Charmingly trite. But your words will not spare you the torture I have planned. You will come sobbing, crawling to me on bloodied knees, begging for release from torment. Loved ones lost to death. Country divided and burning.

Food and money nowhere to be found. I will reduce you to nothing. You will eat one another's flesh in the days to come!

At last you speak a sliver of truth - by accident of course! For God has spoken, 'Whoever eats my flesh and drinks my blood has eternal life, and I will raise them up at the last day.' His sacrifice seals it. In His flesh the debt is paid, the grave is conquered, and His Kingdom is established. Of course, this is the truth you cannot speak, isn't it?

...

Nothing more to say? Very well. Then you'd best be on your way. You have so little time left. What you are about to do, do quickly.

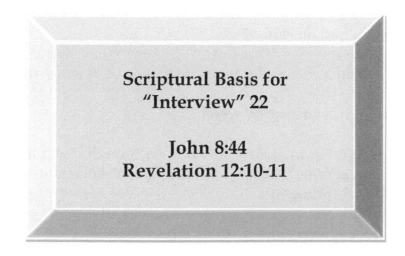

Scriptural Basis for "Interview" 22

**John 8:44
Revelation 12:10-11**

"Interview" 23
Paul

Paul! You have one of the most dramatic conversion stories in history! From trying to burn the Church to the ground to spreading the fire of Christ throughout the known world... How did that go down?

It was a hammer - the hammer of God. And I was a tent peg.

Boom! Just like that, huh?

Laid me out flat. When Jesus confronted me, I instantly fell on my face. The power of His presence was undeniable, and he demanded my unconditional surrender.

So you had no choice?

Oh, I had a choice. But to refuse was to be at war with God.

I thought you already were...

True, but I didn't know it. I honestly thought I was fighting heresy, serving God by squashing this blasphemous sect that had sprung up.

You went after them with a vengeance.

I'm a passionate guy, what can I say?

Are you a fanatic?

I would describe it more as 'all in.'

You bring that same intensity to the tent-making arena?

Very tight stitches, man. Very tight stitches. No - I'm kidding. When it came to making tents I was pretty relaxed. I still worked hard, of course - that work ethic was in my blood - but working with my hands was always very gratifying.

I get that. So when you did finally surrender to Jesus as LORD, how quickly did you start putting the pieces together that he was the One the scriptures were talking about?

Oh, that was fast. And thrilling! For someone like me – a Pharisee who had so much of the Torah memorized – once I saw Yeshua as the Messiah it all started lighting up. Words began leaping from the scroll. Certain phrases from the prophets flared to life. And once you see them all start to connect, their meaning-packed messages arcing through space and time like lightning racing across the clouds in all directions and touching every corner of the sky, it is not long before you realize it's all one story!

You saw the connections that clearly?

It was impossible to miss. I had meticulously studied and cherished all these seemingly unrelated fragments of our history... but now suddenly I was shown this bright common thread running right through the heart of all of them. And the more I went back and reviewed the scriptures the more the pieces slid into place - like a lock when you turn the key.

Ok, now right there... We need to address your descriptive illustrations. You have an undeniable gift for that. 'Run in such a way as to win the prize...' 'Put on the full armor of God...' 'If the whole body were an eye...' Explaining spiritual concepts using examples from athletics or the military or anatomy or music... How do you come up with such effective analogies?

Inspired. I think that's the word you would use. In Hebrew our word for spirit and breath is the same. So when we say we are inspired, we mean that we are filled with the Spirit and also with breath. The Spirit breathes in us. God's breath fills us with life. When you speak, you let that breath come out. That is how Jesus taught, and He says we have access to the same exact source. In fact, he says we can't bear fruit without it. So I spend time with Him. I breathe, and in His presence I am 'inspired.' That's where I find the words.

Last question... you were this horrible persecutor of the Church. You had believers literally running and hiding for their lives. You saw them imprisoned and executed for their faith in Jesus. And then, in a miraculous turn-around, you became a champion of the faith you had

tried to destroy, adding so much, serving so many, and ultimately laying down your own life for the Lord. Do you think we'll ever see another instance of transformation like that, and is there anyone you would love to see come to faith because of the effect they could have?

Everyone! I want to see everyone saved. I know that God uses even His enemies to accomplish His perfect plan, but it is so much fuller when people freely turn and give Him their hearts. And what talents and treasures are hidden in those hearts! It is stunning what God has equipped people to do. As for specific individuals who might follow my path, I think it was significant that I did want to please God, even when I was doing it all wrong. If someone is doing real damage, but that person genuinely wants to do right by God, there is a good chance that it could all turn around. True surrender, scales falling from the eyes, and suddenly our weakness turns to strength. That's how it went for me, and I believe God is always calling in that direction. So yes, I think we could see more dramatic turns like mine, and with earth-shaking results. But there's no telling who it might be. Or when...

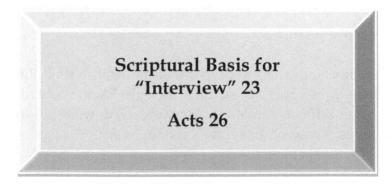

Scriptural Basis for "Interview" 23

Acts 26

"Interview" 24
The Good Son

Big brother, huh?

Yeah. Don't remind me. You have siblings?

I do. Really good ones.

You got lucky then.

Your little brother was kind of a handful?

Not a handful. Just a loser. The selfish bastard took his inheritance while our father was still alive and just left.

Left?

Left our family. Left our fields. Left all the work behind and disappeared.

Where did he go?

You know Vegas? Kind of like that, but without all the flashing lights. Same basic lure, though. Excitement and pleasure. Wine and women. Whatever you want, all for sale. That's where our father's money went.

That made you angry?

Not really. At least he was gone. Good riddance, you know? I wasn't angry until he came back. That's what really pissed me off.

You were angry that he came home?

Home?! He doesn't have a home! That's what it means when you walk out on your family. When you burn through your share of the estate being a total jackass. When you drop your half of the load and leave all the work for your brother.

Hey, I feel you man. So did you kick him out?

I would have.

But...?

My father is alive.

Your father is alive... What does that mean?

It means that I am not the one in charge. The remaining inheritance is mine, but only because I am his. My father is not dead. He lives, and he welcomed his other son back home.

So that is what made you angry? That your father still loves your brother?

No. I wasn't even thinking about it like that. I was only thinking about myself - getting all riled up about what I deserved and what my idiot brother didn't. I was so mad that I wouldn't even go inside and enjoy the amazing feast our father grilled up to welcome him home.

You know you're mad when you refuse to go in and eat!

That's what I'm saying. But then my dad came out...

Your dad came out to you?

Yeah. He put his arm around me and explained it... how his other son was lost - pretty much dead to us - but that he had come back to life because he turned around and came home. It took me a while to cool down, but I get it. My dad really loves his sons. Both of us. I can't fault him for that. Where would I be if he didn't?

So he convinced you to forgive him?

It actually went much deeper... I thought about it a lot after I calmed down, and I eventually ended up feeling pretty convicted about my own position.

As the older brother?

No, as the 'righteous' brother. Look, my brother is a freaking moron. He probably always will be. He wastes most of his life chasing his appetites. But he never wished that I was dead or hoped I would be cast out. He never wanted to see me beaten or punished for my sins. Those are all the things I felt toward him. Hard to admit that, but once I did there was a tough reality to deal with: between me and my brother, which of us was harboring wickedness toward the other?

Wow.

Yeah. Sin is sneaky like that. I am the legitimate son. I am the heir. All that my father has is mine. Everything is gravy. So how did that turn into hatred for my brother?

Dang. Where do you go with that?

Nowhere else to go. Unless I want to kill my brother and hate my father, I have to open the door, head on in, and celebrate that the knucklehead came home.

So no one ends up left outside?

No one who wants to come back... After all, there is plenty of room, the feast is off the charts, and someone bought wedding clothes for everybody.

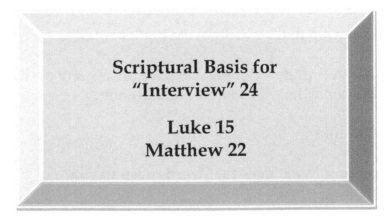

**Scriptural Basis for
"Interview" 24**

**Luke 15
Matthew 22**

"Interview" 25
Job

Everyone talks about your suffering. I want to go in a different direction. Talk to me about restoration.

Just skip the whole part about destruction and loss?

You've probably gone over that before, right?

About a million times.

That's what I figured. We have that part of your story - those truths are out there for us when we need them.

Wait, so you don't want to discuss patience and endurance?

I feel like you have covered those in other places as well.

Yeah... I mean that's usually what I talk about.

And it's definitely valuable. Let's not throw any of that out. But today let's do something different.

Ummm... ok.

Restoration. What does that word mean to you?

Wow. Let's see... Getting your life back. That's the first thing that hits me. Relief. Healing. Coming out of the storm at last. That's what I feel when I hear that word.

Have you experienced that kind of restoration?

I sure have.

What is that like?

Like being able to breathe again. As if there was this crushing weight on my chest and on my arms and legs and right on my face. I could not move it and it sat on me for years, pressing the life out of me minute by minute as the hours and days and months crawled by. But eventually, finally, that seemingly endless season was complete and the crushing weight was lifted off.

That weight is gone?

I still remember it. I can even go back and visit that place I was in, almost like a museum. But it's not on me anymore.

You can breathe...

I can breathe! Whew... And hope! That is huge. I have hope again! For a while there I didn't. I didn't hope for anything except for the crushing weight to finish the job and end the suffering. But there was no real hope for life. I was too afraid of that.

Afraid to hope?

117

Yes. Hope only led to more pain when things didn't get better, and I could not take one more sliver of pain. So I refused to allow hope any room. Despair was welcome to come in and sit, but the door was locked against hope. Restoration has gradually switched that back the other way.

Ah, so now despair is locked out...

Most of the time. I still have to guard the door, but at least now I have the strength to let hope in again. It's much better this way.

I bet. So what caused the shift? When did restoration start?

This is a tough one to swallow, but the truth is worth telling... In our self-centered understanding of the world, we want it to be a 'I finally got it, surrendered to God, and flipped the switch' moment. But it isn't always like that. Sometimes it is a 'I am on the workbench and the craftsman is going to take that chisel to my heart until the job is done' kind of thing.

So there is no control over how long that season lasts or when it happens?

None. Well... maybe not none. We may do things that influence it. I don't know. What I do know is that when you are in it you are desperate to exert some sort of control, but those efforts do no good. You can squirm on the table as much as you want. The doctor is in no hurry. He will wait. There is definitely a timetable, though. It's just none of our business.

So back to the question at hand... when does restoration start?

When it's time.

That's not very reassuring.

It isn't, and yet it is. We don't like suffering, and we don't like being unable to control how long it lasts. But I am not sure that there is anything *MORE* reassuring than the fact that restoration is definitely, irresistibly, undeniably coming. If you want control over how and when, you are right - you are going to be frustrated. But if you just want to know that restoration is God's plan, well you can lay back into that right now. That's not selfish, and it's not you wrestling for control. That is trust. And the One who promises our restoration is worthy of our trust. Every time.

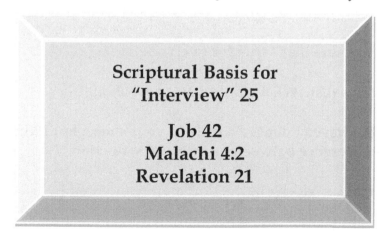

Scriptural Basis for "Interview" 25

Job 42
Malachi 4:2
Revelation 21

"Interview" 26
Daughter of Herodias

If you know how to dress it up, you can get their attention. If you know how to move it, you can get what you want... It's that simple.

Where did you learn that?

Mother.

Your *mother* taught you that?!

If she didn't, someone would have. Everyone knows that's how it works.

Do you think all women resort to those kinds of tactics?

The ugly ones don't. But if you've got it, you flaunt it.

I'm not sure that's true for everyone.

You're a man. What would you know about it?

Well, I haven't danced a mile in your shoes, but I know the difference between beauty and seduction.

Oh really? Which one are you more influenced by?

On my best days? Beauty.

And on your worst days?

I've definitely fallen for the seductive before. But that doesn't mean seduction is beautiful. It just means sometimes I'm stupid.

You and every other man. That's why it works.

What do you think the cost is to you?

The cost? I get what I want. That's the cost.

I mean long term. What is the long term cost to your heart?

I don't have the luxury of thinking that way. I am a woman living in a world dominated by men. I do what I have to do to survive.

Is it survival, though? Because what you said was 'I get what I want.'

Same thing. You pursue what you want, don't you?

It depends. Sometimes God calls us to forgo what we want in the moment. Other times he calls us to trust him for what we need, rather than trying to get it the wrong way.

Well I don't need anything from a god referred to as 'him' and I don't need a lecture from you. I thought this was supposed to be an interview.

You're right. Sorry. Questions only. What was the last thing you received for dancing?

What...?

What was the last thing that you were given by a man because you danced in a way that enticed him sexually?

Hey, I don't like your tone.

My tone or the question?

Both.

OK, I'll change my tone. What did you earn the last time you danced?

I think you know.

You don't want to say it?

Nah, I don't care.

What was it?

It doesn't matter.

Is it what you wanted?

No... I should have asked for something better. I got caught up in the moment and I wasn't sure what to do. So I asked my mother. I should have known she was going to tell me to ask for something bad. She's really spiteful and insecure, especially when she drinks.

What did you ask for?

She used me, ok. It's not like I wanted it. I should have asked for something better.

What was it?

Why do you keep asking that?

Because you haven't answered yet. Are you ashamed?

Hell no! You can't judge me.

Then what was it?

Some guy's head, ok? My mother wanted it. The king said I could have whatever I wanted and my mother said to ask for that. It was stupid. I should have asked for something better.

Like what?

Anything. Anything would have been better than that. Next time I'm asking for cash.

You're dancing again?

Of course. These jewels on my neck aren't free.

Are you sure that's who you want to be? There is actual beauty in you. You know that, right? God created you with immeasurable value. You are made in His image. You could cultivate that instead.

Yeah? How much are you going to pay me to be nice?

Not everything is about money.

Says a man who can get any job he wants.

That's not true, though. We all have limits – everyone has to make hard choices.

Well I choose to dance. Necklaces look good on me.

Some necklaces are just pretty shackles.

Was that a question?

No. Let's end with this one: if the God who created you and loves you was in the room, sitting there at the table with all the dinner guests, would you dance the same way?

Hey, take it easy. I don't need the moral interrogation. It's not like I ever killed anybody...

Scriptural Basis for "Interview" 26

Mark 6 : 14-28
Proverbs 31 : 30

"Interview" 27
The Barn Builder

Check out my house! Brand new. Just had it built. Six car garage. Imported marble.

I thought you lived in Virginia.

I do. I mean, that's my first house. That's where the kids live. I've got a really nice vacation home in the Outer Banks as well, and a luxury cabin up on Lake Minnetonka, so we have a few places to go and play. Of course, with this new place finished, I am clearly going to need to spend a little more time in Florida. Have to do some extensive golf course research, if you know what I mean.

Wow. That's a lot of property.

Real estate is where it's at, man. You should really get into it, I mean if you're serious about your finances. There is no more reliable investment you can make. Build, man, build! I'm already closing on another property in San Diego.

Isn't it expensive out there?

Not as expensive as my second wife! Ha. If it weren't for her, I'd still have the place in the Hamptons. And the boat!

How does all that fit in with your medical condition?

What medical condition?

The tests came back. I thought you knew. You've got 12 hours.

12 hours for what? What happens then?

I'm not sure how else to say it... that's the end. Time's up.

Time for what? What are you talking about?

We're all given a certain number of days. You are on your last one.

Yeah, right. I've got insurance.

That's not going to help. There's no treatment for this.

There's always treatment. I can fly a doctor in from anywhere in the world.

You sure can. If that's how you want to spend your last day, you should probably get on it.

I don't think you understand who you are talking to. I have more money than god! I own senators. I write laws in my dining room. There is not a car I can't buy or a woman I can't have. My name is on buildings in twelve major cities! You don't just take down a man like me.

Let me ask you a question... Can you tell me the first names of your great-great grandparents?

Who?

Your great-great grandparents. Not mine. Yours. You have sixteen of them. Direct relatives, four generations back. How many of their first names do you know?

Can you picture any of their faces? Do you know what their favorite song was or what they liked to eat? Have you heard about the hardest time in their lives? Can you share the most important thing they ever learned?

... no.

That's how time works. It buries us even deeper than the dirt. I asked about your own family, and the truth is you couldn't pick them out of a crowd. Most people can't. It will be the same with you. Just three generations from now, no one on the planet will know you were even here.

Most people don't have my kind of success. I've built an empire! I've got enough saved up to live like a king for a hundred years.

Congratulations. But who is going to get all that? By this time tomorrow your body will be on the slab. Your houses will be auctioned off, your estate divided, and all your money scattered to the winds. One imported marble headstone and a footnote in a genealogical research project by one of your great grandkids will be the last fading echoes of your life. Then silence. The world will spin on, leaving you behind. That is reality. That's the truth.

But you can't do that. Look around. I have it all!

And tomorrow you will stand and give an account of exactly what you did with it. Your final interview...

Wait! Please... What will they ask?

They will ask what you did with all that you were given.

To see if I was good enough?

No. To see which god you loved.

Scriptural Basis for "Interview" 27

Luke 12 : 13-21
1 Peter 1 : 23-25

"Interview" 28
Michael

Was there really war in Heaven?

Yes. There was.

Maybe I shouldn't be fascinated by that, but I'm kind of fascinated by that! I keep wondering what it looked like.

Like nothing you have ever seen.

Oh, I have so many questions! What kinds of weapons do angels use? Do you fight in the air or on the ground? Is the battlefield crystal clear, or choked with smoke and fire?

You are trying to use earthly images.

That's all I have.

It's not going to work. What you are asking about goes far beyond the physical.

Beyond the physical?

Consider this! Don't rush past it. Take a moment to realize this is true: Your physical body does not go to war of its own volition, as if it was driving itself. The body goes to war under the command of the one inside it. Do you understand this? You are not your body - you DRIVE your body.

Like a tank?

You're kind of squishy to think of yourself as a tank.

Hurtful...

But yes - your body is a vehicle. You are spirit. The spirit steers. The physical responds. As it is with the individual, so it is with humanity as a whole. Your spirits steer reality. Reality responds. With every physical war on earth there is an unseen spiritual conflict going on underneath.

But I can't picture that.

This is why it is so difficult for you to imagine war in Heaven. But you can be sure of this - earthly wars begin a long time before the shooting starts.

Oh, we know that! Politicians making decisions with other people's lives? Propagandists in the media who manipulate emotions to serve their own ends? We're well aware of the problem.

No, you are well aware of the symptoms! The real problem is much deeper. War is, at its root, an issue of the heart, and you are under attack by powers that you cannot see, powers that are constantly vying for control of your heart. That is the deeper battle, and it is occurring all the time.

Nations rise and fall, but human hearts are eternal. Spiritual territory is forever.

So the war is inside, not outside?

It's both. The sword is very real. Bullets aren't imaginary. But picking up the sword in the first place is a heart decision. Your highest virtues and lowest vices as people are all a result of what happens in the heart - what you choose to trust, what you give yourself to on a daily basis. That internal battle is much more like war in Heaven than bombs and bullets are.

How do you fight that kind of war? I'm just being honest here... it's really hard to know what the sides are. People are shouting all kinds of things, and a lot of it just sounds like self-important noise.

That is the center of the battle - it gets loud. The Enemy plants lies like IED's and tries to convince everyone that they are the center of truth in the universe. A few heated arguments here and there, and division spreads among the ranks. It's the same strategy he's been using since the beginning – the same tactics he used to launch the war in Heaven. But not everything that people believe is right actually is. Not everything is of the LORD. This is why faith is so key. You are fighting a war that you can't see - one that a lot of you aren't even aware of. You all know some sort of conflict is happening, and you do have a vague awareness of good and evil, but your understanding of spiritual things is limited. It's not a fair fight, and it all occurs beyond the limits of physical sight.

Then what are we supposed to do?

Listen. Here it is... Love the LORD your God with all your heart, soul, strength and mind, and love your neighbor as yourself. That's it. That's where you discover that you aren't actually fighting on your own. That is where you learn that God is fighting FOR you. And that's where you win spiritual battles. Despite the noise and confusion, your orders actually haven't changed. Love God with all you are. Love other people - and yourself.

That doesn't sound like war.

Really? How often are you able to do it?

...

Right. Pay attention to that. If you are unable to do what God commands – even things that you recognize as being right – then there is something going on. That is the war beneath the war, and it happens in the heart.

OK, let's start to wrap this up with a little clarification... It has been written that we should fight the good fight of faith, resist the devil and he will flee from us, and put on the full armor of God. But how do we actually DO these things? How do we put on armor that's not even real?!

Whoa... careful there! It is not *physical*. But the armor and weapons of the spirit are very real, and many of you are running around the battlefield naked and unarmed. It looks ridiculous to us, but we know you cannot see. Still, it is not completely beyond you. You have been told that your battle is not against flesh and blood, but against unseen powers and principalities. Arm up accordingly. Love when it is hard. Love with actions and self-sacrifice. Love when and how God's Spirit moves. After all, you have no real power without Him! So ask God to equip and supply you. That's how you put the armor on. Stop pretending to "love" by adding more empty words to the noise. Do not "love" in ways that are secretly designed to exalt yourself. And do not lend yourselves to fight for the enemy. Hear that again... Don't aid those spiritual forces trying to divide and destroy you (both individually and as God's people). Fighting against yourself is terrible military strategy, and some of you are doing it all the time.

I must admit, I'm pretty overwhelmed by the whole thing. It's confusing. It's daunting. How do we even start? There is already so much brokenness. The enemy already has so much territory. It seems hopeless. I feel defeated just thinking about it.

That is what the enemy wants. That is his only chance. Because if you actually look to the LORD and see who He truly is, you will realize that the one inside you is infinitely greater than the one attacking you. Infinitely. It's not even close. So seek Jesus on the front line and jump on in beside Him. He holds even the angels in His hand! And don't be in awe of firepower or the size of armies or stockpiles of resources, for human power is not what determines the outcome. As it is in Heaven, it will be on earth. The battle belongs to the LORD.

Scriptural Basis for "Interview" 28

Revelation 12
Ephesians 6 : 10-17
1 John 4 : 4
Psalm 20 : 7
Psalm 144:1
1 Samuel 17:47

"Interview" 29
Amnon

What was she wearing?

Oh man, you should have see-

Stop right there. What she was wearing is no excuse for what you did.

Oh, I see what this is. You bring me in here to grill me...

Grill you? No - that would do no good.

What then? Why am I here?

You're here because your story is still relevant. I wish it wasn't. It's a mark on men everywhere that this still happens, but it's an evil that we need to face.

Fine. You said it. Can I go now?

Did you let *HER* go?

...

No. You didn't. You schemed and trapped and raped her. That's what happened. And it still happens. So tell us - what made you think it was ok?

I wanted to have her. That desire was all I thought about. All day, every day. I wasn't paying attention to whether or not it was ok.

Well pay attention now. I don't want us to miss anything...
King David was your father - is that right?

Yes.

And which of his sons were you? Third, fourth, fifth?

I was the first.

Wait - you?!! You were the firstborn son of David, king of Israel?

Yes.

You know what that means... you were the heir! The next in line for -

- the throne, I know. Don't remind me.

You would have been King of Israel, and during some of Israel's best days! But instead of that, instead of being remembered as the successor to your father David, what you are famous for is being a rapist.

Thanks for putting it that way.

Can't say you weren't warned... What did Tamar say would happen if you raped her?

She said that I would become one of the wicked fools of Israel.

Pretty much nailed it, didn't she? Instead of 'Amnon, King of Israel' you end up being 'Amnon, wicked fool of Israel.' That's a pretty long fall. You lost the throne, your honor, and the love of your family all in one move. It even got you killed, too, didn't it?

I suppose, if you want to get technical...

Oh I do. Let's get technical. If you had NOT raped Tamar, then her brother would not have executed you for it. Is that the kind of technical you mean?

Look, haven't you ever been attracted to someone? I mean, like crazy attracted? What was I supposed to do?

Not raping her would be a good start.

Obviously. I clearly let it get out of control.

Was it ever in control?

I don't know. I would see her around. She was so beautiful. So full of life. I wanted her more than anything.

What do you mean, you wanted her?

I don't think I even knew at first. I just wanted to be close to her. But the closer I got the more I wanted. It was so frustrating. I could never get close enough. So I started to fantasize in my mind about what we would do if we were alone. I imagined enjoying her body, and I never got free of that. I thought about it all the time, and it just got worse and worse. It was like being hungry, but much more exciting, and every time I saw her that hunger got stronger. I had to have her, to possess her.

You never stopped to consider whether it was right to fantasize about her that way?

I told myself it didn't matter. It wasn't real. It was just a fantasy. It was only in my mind.

Until it wasn't.

Yeah. A friend of mine figured out a way for me to get her alone.

Some friend...

Right. Though he didn't have to work too hard to convince me. I was already way down that road in my heart.

So it wasn't just a fantasy anymore at that point?

No. At that point it was a plan.

But not a plan to love her. Not a plan to care about her. Not a plan to do anything good for her at all, right? Be honest - what was the point of the plan?

To take her. It was a trap. That's what it was. I wanted her so bad I didn't care how I got her.

Even if she said no?

Didn't even consider it.

Even if she tried to push you away?

She wouldn't be able to. I was a strong guy.

Even if you hurt her?

Don't you get it? It wasn't about her. It was about what I wanted.

And you chased that desire right off a cliff. You lost everything.

Yes.

And you destroyed her in the process.

Yes.

And you got killed for it.

Yes.

Did you get anything good from all that?

No. The pleasure turned putrid instantly. I felt empty and sick. All the fondness and attraction I had for her turned to hate. I just wanted her gone, so I had her thrown out.

There is nothing good about that.

No. Nothing.

For all the men here, level with us - you lost the war when you raped her, but the battle started a long time before that, didn't it?

A really long time before. In fact, I think the war was lost before the rape. Could I have risen up in some last second heroic moment of self-denial? How? I had been practicing to lose the war every day in my mind. How could I expect to reverse all that in the heat of the moment? No. The rape was the snapping of the trap, but I lost the war through months and years of cultivation - a thousand little wicked thoughts when no one was around. It started with a look. But then I looked again. And again. And soon I was looking with evil intent. I did not defend the territory in my heart and mind. I did not love God. I did not love her. I did not even love myself.

That's the most honest thing you've said all day. Thank you for that.

Warn the men. It is not too late to turn and fight. Warn them! Tell them where it starts. Call them higher. Don't let them end up here with me. It's horrible on this side. I lost it all. I hate myself.

As you wish...

When asked about sex trafficking, a lot of guys imagine themselves kicking in the door to a room full of little girls being held prisoner by perverts. They raise their imaginary machine guns and spray bullets until every last rapist scum bag is a permanent part of the back wall.

But these same guys then go home and click through image after image and video after video, financing the entire industry. They pretend it doesn't matter because it isn't real. But it is real. The only thing that is not real is the daydream about kicking down the door of the sex-traffickers' lair and saving the kids.

The good news is that there is one potential sex-abuser we each have access to on a daily basis, one man whose heart we can fight for on behalf of women everywhere. It's that guy in the mirror. He's not Rambo. He's not going to single-handedly eradicate sexual abuse, but he can surrender his own sexuality to God and fight against pornography and infidelity like he's fighting for his life - and for his wife. He's not going to free every kidnapped little girl, but decreasing the demand decreases the number of victims, including his own daughters and sons. There are no harmless little clicks. There is no healthy fantasy that is not about your wife.

Take it from Amnon. He should have been the king.

**Scriptural Basis for
"Interview" 29**

**2 Samuel 13
2 Samuel 3 : 2
Matthew 5 : 27-28
Job 31 : 1**

"Interview" 30
Noah

First of all, please let me apologize for the scheduling issues. I meant to have you on earlier, but this current pandemic has everything upside down and backward.

It's affecting a lot of things?

You have no idea. It's a global disaster of epic proportions, the size and scope of which the world has never seen!

Fascinating. Say, I heard about your quarantine. How long have you been in lockdown?

Over four months now! Well, kind of. We've had breaks...

Four months? Rookies...

Hey man. What would you know about it? I read your story. You were only trapped for forty days and forty nights. We've tripled that!

You might need to go back and read it again. It RAINED for forty days and forty nights. It was an entire year before we were able to step outside and leave the ark.

A year?

That's right... No going for a walk, either. Or sneaking to the grocery store just to get out of the house for an hour. There were no breaks. Just us and the animals in the boat for twelve months.

Oh... wow. How did you survive that?

Same way you do. Get up. Do the day. Go to sleep. Repeat.

Weren't you stir-crazy? Weren't you dying to go outside?

People outside *were* dying. That was the point. I don't know what the fatality rate is for the plague you are facing, but the flood basically wiped out 100% of the world population. Every human life on the planet, gone... except the eight of us. We were it. The only survivors on the face of the earth.

That had to be surreal. What is it like to be alone on a planet?

I can't describe that. There aren't words.

Come on... there has to be something.

Let's see – ok, one thing I do remember is how silent it was.

Silent?

The raging, thundering, screaming voice of humanity was completely cut off in an instant. And what followed was silence. Such sweet silence. The earth could breathe again.

What do you mean by that?

Before we got on the ark it was loud. The noise of mankind was an endless roar. Arrogant, boastful, violent. To put it bluntly, humanity was gross - wicked to the point of being both repulsive and terrifying. You can feel that kind of evil all around you. It saturates the air to the point where you can hear it even when no one is talking. It was so angry, suffocating, deafening... and that noise had filled the earth. After the flood all of that noise was gone. It was so silent – so peaceful.

The calm after the storm?

The calm after a war.

War?

It was obvious... people had been at war with their creator. Every lie and murder was an attack on God. Every theft and rape was an invasion, an assault on what He had made. For centuries, men and women forced their way across the map, taking ground and establishing cities that churned out more and more evil. When men and women choose to actively hate God it gets really bad. People were awful to each other. It was a terrible place to live.

And then?

Then God fired back. Just once. That was all it took. We saw first-hand how completely effortless it is for God to wage war on mankind.

What did you see?

Overwhelming victory. When we stepped off the ark, the stench of evil had been swept off the field. Everything was clean. Everything was at peace. Then God hung up his bow. One shot. No more. He set his bow in the sky as a lasting promise that He would never fight that way again.

No more global flood?

He had a better answer already in motion, one He had in mind since the beginning.

A better answer?

Destroying the world is easy. Even man can do that. Saving it... now that is something else entirely.

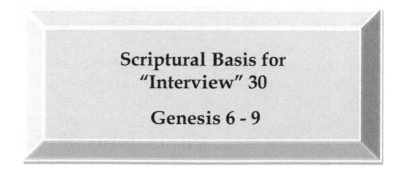

Scriptural Basis for "Interview" 30

Genesis 6 - 9

"Interview" 31
Moses

You must be Moses.

What gave me away? The veil? The shining face?

No. You're my last appointment of the afternoon.

Ah, right...

I'm going to level with you – I'm a little star-struck. On my list of people to interview, you're kind of a heavy hitter. There aren't many folks out there who have face to face conversations with God.

The heart to heart is more important than the face to face.

Good point. Still, you stand out. There are a million things I would love to ask you about, but there is one question in particular that I want to make sure we get to.

Is it about the plagues? The waters of the Red Sea standing on end? Meeting with God at the top of Mount Sinai to receive the Law?

No... I wanted to ask if you feel like God ripped you off.

Ripped me off? What do you mean?

Your life was not easy. You were called to do some really challenging things – to step out in faith again and again. Not only did you confront Pharaoh and lead a huge group of people out of slavery toward the Promised Land, but then you had to govern those grumbling people in the desert for nearly half a century after they proved faithless.

There were some challenging seasons in my life, no doubt about that, but I think that's true of just about everybody. That's where the growing happens.

Sure, but after you went through all those difficult seasons, God takes you right to the edge of the Promised Land – the place you have been straining toward the whole time – only to let you look into it and die without crossing over. Now, we know that there was a reason for that. The Bible clearly states why you weren't allowed to enter. But don't you feel like you got cheated a little bit?

I suppose that's how it might look. Like he led me all that way only to drop me at the end? Like he used me and then pushed me aside because I didn't live up to an unrealistic standard of perfection? Like he cheated me?

That's exactly how it looks. So how ticked off were you? Are you still angry about that?

Angry? No. You have to understand... That was mercy.

Mercy... How is it mercy to *NOT* be allowed to cross over into the land God promised to Abraham?

Do you remember what happened to the people who crossed over into Canaan? Their struggles were just beginning! It wasn't all sunshine and puppies over there waiting for them. They were heading into battle – literally – and that was just the physical part. The spiritual challenges they had to face were even harder. No, Israel didn't enter Paradise when they crossed over into the Promised Land. They entered into the next stage of their walk with God, a walk designed for their growth. I don't want to sound like a complainer, but I'd had more than enough by then.

You mean that after all your labor and faithful following, you were fine with not receiving your reward?

Reward? Oh, the land was not my reward. God has much bigger things than that for us! Unbounded friendship with God... That is what I was longing for. That was the purpose of the journey. The Real Promise is entering back into a healed relationship with our Creator, not a new chunk of ground to walk around on.

So you weren't angry?

Was I angry when God smiled at me, wrapped his arms around me, and finally said, 'Good job. Come home'? No. Not at all. I took my last breath with a smile on my face. Relieved of duty. Embraced by God. Finally being allowed to see what it was all for. And then He led me home into real power and freedom. That was perfect. That was the reward I was craving. I had no desire to be king over all those people or continue to judge their disputes. I was striving toward the same thing your heart strives toward – something beyond this world and its burdens. And at the end of my earthly wanderings, God was there to complete the story. He was faithful to me, and I was glad to go, because the border I really longed to cross was not the one that led into Canaan, but the one that led into life.

And you have that now?

You bet I do. Read that whole Mount of Transfiguration account again. That is me now. Restored, happy, and home.

So your death at the border wasn't a defeat?

No. It was the finish line! There is no need for bitter tears or hopeless wailing over God-loving men and women who take that next step. Raise a glass instead, celebrate and cheer as if they just won a marathon, and then forge on in your own walk with the Lord. You'll see us on the other side!

Scriptural Basis for "Interview" 31

**Deuteronomy 34
Mark 9**

"Interview" 32

Joshua

I got to chat with your predecessor in the last interview.

Moses stopped by, did he? Now that is one remarkable man! Someone in his exalted position who is able to remain truly humble? So rare! It was an honor to serve under and learn from him. What did you ask him about?

About him not being allowed to enter the Promised Land.

Oh! There is such deep meaning there!

Meaning? As in Moses being punished for a moment of failure in leadership?

Much deeper than that.

The Bible says he was not allowed to enter the land because he -

I know what it says... I was there.

Are you telling me that it wasn't about him breaking faith with God?

Oh, it was... God is not a liar. The breach of faith at the second rock happened. At the same time, you have to look at the whole story or you are going to miss it!

Miss what? What deeper meaning are you talking about?

There is only one way for you to see it. What does Moses represent? Can you tell me that?

What do you mean?

Moses' life, his journey – what is the one thing he ends up being most connected with? Is it baptism?

Well, they did cross through the waters of the Red Sea...

Yes! Baptism is there. Is that the dominant theme throughout his journey?

Not really. There are other people more closely tied to baptism.

What then? What is Moses linked to? Is it the cross?

Well, there is the snake on a pole...

Good. You caught that. The cross is definitely there. And it is hidden within the Passover as well. But is the cross what Moses is most closely associated with?

That's not typically what comes to mind.

Then what? If there is one huge piece of God's journey with humanity that is more connected to Moses than to anyone else, what would it be?

I guess it would have to be the Law.

You got it! Moses is chosen by God to deliver the Law and then guide His people in following it – so much so that throughout the rest of the Bible, whenever they talk about 'reading Moses' they are talking about reading the Law.

So Moses is the Law?

Symbolically, yes. Now think... how does that apply to your question about Moses not being allowed to enter the Promised Land? Do you see it?

See what?

Moses not being able to lead the people over is an enormous thing! It is one of the deepest truths that God has revealed.

Which is...

The Law cannot get you there.

Oh... wait!

You see it now? Moses could not lead the people into the Promised Land because the Law cannot lead us into the deeper promise that the land symbolizes.

The deeper promise...?

The real promise we are moving to is Heaven, which is not some ethereal cartoon with angels sitting on clouds playing harps. Heaven is what exists when creation is in a restored, perfect relationship with God. No more sin, no more pain, no more death, and ESPECIALLY no more separation from Him. That is Heaven – and we can only enter that perfect place if we are made perfect ourselves. The Law cannot do that. It cannot make us right with God.

It can take us to the border...

But it can't cross over. The Law reveals about us exactly what God said to Moses. "You did not trust me enough to honor me as holy." What God states there – read carefully – is the human condition since the Fall, when we did not trust God enough to honor Him as holy (at the tree)! So the Law takes us up the mountain to get a clear view of the barrier that exists between us and God because of our broken relationship. Yet even though we can see our sin because of the Law, it cannot help us cross over. A healing, a cleansing, a baptism is required, and the Law can't do that. It only exposes sin; it is powerless to forgive it.

So that whole interaction... it was about more than just a punishment of Moses for a moment of failure.

Of course it was. God is not petty or vindictive. He is doing an incredible, beautiful thing, and His journey with Moses is used to reveal a central piece of it.

Okay, I can see how Moses being stopped at the border is a clear communication of the limits of the Law. But where is the beautiful part? Where is the hope?

That's where I come in. Like Moses, I was chosen to play a role in this stunning picture of salvation – a revelation of what God is ultimately doing to bring us all home. You have asked about the deeper meaning and you have asked about hope. They are both here. For when the Law was stopped by death, that's where Moses' mission ended and mine began. You see, I got to lead them in!

You?

'Be strong and courageous,' is the charge I was given. 'Be strong and very courageous.' And why was I given such a bold command? Because my mission symbolized the real one that God had in mind – the heart of it all. There could be no shrinking back!
Pay attention to the details…
In order to cross over, there was a baptism required at the Jordan. Sound familiar yet? There was no other way across. Through that baptism the barrier split – the separation was removed – and we crossed over to the place that had been promised, the place we had left long before, the place we had been journeying toward for so long…

You took them where the Law could not.

Yes! Marching to victory, demolishing ancient strongholds to the sound of trumpets, declaring freedom for the captives… Can you see it? Can you see me leading God's people home?

Yes. I can see that. But why you? Why Joshua?

Don't you know? What's my name?

Scriptural Basis for "Interview" 32

Numbers 20:12
Joshua 3 - 6
Matthew 1 : 21

"Thy word
is a lamp unto my feet
and a light unto my path"

Psalm 119

brianwallacebooks.com

Made in the USA
Middletown, DE
19 September 2020